LUTHERAN
HIGH SCHOOL
RELIGION SERIES ®

One Body in Christ

A Study of the Church

Student Book

By James Klawiter

Edited by Board for Parish Services Staff
Editor: Arnold E. Schmidt

CONCORDIA

Publishing House
St. Louis

Editorial Secretary: Phoebe Wellman

Write to Library for the Blind, 1333 S. Kirkwood Road, St. Louis, MO 63122-7295 to obtain *One Body in Christ* (Student Book) in Braille or sightsaving print for the visually impaired.

Unless otherwise stated, the Scripture quotations in this publication are from The Holy Bible: NEW INTERNATIONAL VERSION, © 1973, 1978, 1984 by the International Bible Society. Used by permission of Zondervan Bible Publishers.

Bible quotations marked RSV are from the Revised Standard Version of the Bible, copyrighted 1946, 1952, © 1971, 1973 by the Division of Christian Education of the National Council of the Churches of Christ in the U.S.A., and are used by permission.

Bible quotations marked TEV are from the Good News Bible, the Bible in TODAY'S ENGLISH VERSION. Copyright © American Bible Society 1966, 1971, 1976. Used by permission.

Scripture quotations marked *NASB* are from the NEW AMERICAN STANDARD BIBLE, © The Lockman Foundation 1960, 1962, 1963, 1968, 1971, 1973, 1975, and are used by permission.

Copyright © 1986 Concordia Publishing House
3558 S. Jefferson Avenue, St. Louis, MO 63118-3968

Contents

To the Student

Do you know?

You started as one cell, but now consist of trillions of cells. Each day about 2 billion cells wear out and are replaced.

Every 15 to 30 days your body replaces the outer layer of skin.

Hair on your head grows as much as 6 inches per year.

By the time you reach age 70, your heart will have pumped at least 46 million gallons of blood.

Messages travel along your nerves at speeds up to 100 yards per second.

You have about 206 bones and 650 muscles. If you weigh 110 pounds, you have about 4 quarts of blood.

More than 100,000 nerves in the retina of an eye send messages to your brain.

Your heart is linked by 100,000 miles of arteries and veins to all parts of the body. It weighs less than 1 pound, is as big as a fist, and beats more than 100,000 times a day. Your heart pumps 5 quarts of blood every 60 seconds. It does enough work in one hour to lift a weight of 1½ tons more than 1 foot off the ground.

God gave you quite a body, didn't He? You probably agree with David, who wrote, **"I praise You because I am fearfully and wonderfully made"** (Psalm 139:14).

Things you know about your human body can help you understand some things God tells you about His church. He inspired Paul, the writer of many epistles in the New Testament, to compare the church to a human body. One time Paul wrote:

"Just as each of us has one body with many members, and these members do not all have the same function, so in Christ we who are many form one body, and each member belongs to all the others" (Romans 12:4-5).

May God bless you as you learn more about your body in Christ!

UNIT 1:

What the Church Is

St. Paul was not an athlete. In fact, he may have been physically disabled. Yet he knew about athletes, particularly those who participated in track and field, and he used track and field as an example of the Christian life.

St. Paul had a deep interest in the church of Jesus Christ. He was Jesus' prime missionary to the Gentiles in the first century A.D. He wrote letters to build up the faith of those who read them. You might think of St. Paul as a spiritual coach and trainer.

St. Paul's letters are also for you—young members of the church. In this course we will read what St. Paul had to say about the church and its purpose—to spread the Word of God and build up the faith of the believers in Jesus Christ.

To help you understand God's plan to make you spiritually strong, you'll find an athletic theme throughout this course. Each session in the first four units is divided into three parts: **Stretching**—a time to loosen up your thinking and to focus on the practice plan. **Getting the Word**—a time to listen as God, through St. Paul, teaches some ideas about the church. **Practice**—a time when you can try out these ideas with your classmates or by yourself.

But what is there to learn about the church? Isn't it enough to know that Jesus Christ died and rose from the dead to assure you of forgiveness and eternal life?

Yes, the Gospel does assure each person of his or her salvation. But Paul rarely speaks to individuals. He usually uses plural pronouns: *you, we, us, them, those, they.* Through Paul we discover that Christ did not save only you or me. **Christ died for all!**

So it's time to look around and discover others who want fellowship with other Christians!

In this first unit you will discover who these others are, what God calls them, and what He has in mind for all of us.

God's blessings of understanding and growth will follow you as you accompany St. Paul.

SESSION 1

God Created It

STRETCHING

Gerry raced to the bulletin board, looking for the big news. Where was the announcement? Finally she saw it—much too small, she thought. Gerry held her breath as she read: "The following have been selected for the girls' varsity basketball team. Please report to the gym immediately after school for an important meeting."

Then followed the most important part, *the list.* It contained the names of the 12 athletes who would represent the school for the season. Right now being on that list was the most important thing in the world to Gerry.

Her eyes scanned down the list frantically until they stopped on the name—her name. **Gordon.** She made it! She made the varsity basketball team! Her feet barely touched the floor as she drifted away in ecstasy.

She was one of the special ones, one of only 12, one who would be a part of *the team.* Just imagine—Gerry Gordon—a member of the varsity basketball team!

Has something like this ever happened to you? What was it?

Maybe you've never made a varsity team, but you have been chosen for a much more important team. The team is called the church. You might be surprised to find out why being on this team is so very important.

Together with your class and your teacher, read **Ephesians 1:1-22.** Find out about this team—the church.

GETTING THE WORD
Ephesians 1:1-2

1. Here you find the names you need to know about in order to understand this section.

a. **Paul:** The last chosen apostle, now (about A. D. 62) in prison in Rome. He was writing to a group of Christians living in Ephesus.

b. **The saints in Ephesus:** A group of Christians living in and around Ephesus, an important seaport of Asia Minor. Some of the group were Jewish, and some were Gentiles. All were called "saints," defined as "the faithful in Christ Jesus." Notice that saints, as Paul uses the word, refers to living, everyday people—people who are full of faith in Jesus, the promised Savior.

c. **God our Father:** Not only the powerful ruler, creator, and avenger of wrong, but also our loving Father, who gives undeserved kindness (grace) and real peace to His children.

d. **Lord Jesus Christ:** the One who made it all possible. *Lord* equates Him with God; Jesus is truly God's Son. *Jesus* means Savior, the One who became true man to save us from sin, death, and the devil. *Christ* shows that He is our king—the Chosen One, the Messiah, the Anointed One.

Be ready to share other information you know about the above.

2. Notice Paul's greeting in **verse 2.** What greeting might you use with other Christians?

_____

Verses 3-14

1. What type of pronouns did Paul use to refer to believers? Why do you think he chose these pronouns?

_____

2. a. List the verbs that show God's action.

_____

b. List the verbs that show our action.

_____

c. What do these verbs show?

_____

3. Notice God's actions in the following chart. After each action tell when God does it.

Action	When Done
a. blessed us (**verse 3**)	_____
b. chose us (**verse 4**)	_____
c. predestined us to be adopted (**verse 5**)	_____
d. redeemed us (**verse 7**)	_____
e. forgives us (**verse 7**)	_____
f. makes His mysteries known to us (**verse 9**)	_____

g. brings all things
   together in Christ
   (**verse 10**) _____

Due to our limited mental capacity, we have to think of each separately in time. But God is not bound by time. He therefore views all 7 actions as a unit.

Because we today hear of God's love in Christ **(f),** we know from the list that God also chose us from eternity **(b).** And as sure as we are of Christ's death **(d),** we are also sure of being eternally gathered together with Him **(g).**

Verses 15-22

1. Paul prayed for the Ephesians. What did he pray for?

_____

_____

2. What mighty acts did God do through Christ?

_____

_____

3. What synonym did Paul use for the church?

_____

4. The Greek word for church is *ecclesia.* It means "a called-out group." How does this fit with **verses 3-14?** How does the introductory story illustrate being one who is called out?

PRACTICE

1. We have talked about a lot of words. What do they mean?

grace _____

Paul _____

saints _____

Ephesus _____

Jesus _____

Lord _____

Christ _____

predestinate _____

church _____

2. Fill out this questionnaire. If you cannot supply all the information now, get it as soon as possible.

Date of Baptism _____

Name of Church Where Baptized _____

Name of Pastor _____

Names of Sponsors _____

_____

Date of Confirmation _____

Name of Congregation Joined _____

Name of Pastor _____

Confirmation Verse _____

_____

Name of Congregation Attended Now _____

3. In this book "church" will sometimes mean the "community of called-out ones." At other times "church" will refer to a group of people organized into a congregation. To show that you can tell the difference, write *called-out ones, congregation,* or *both* before each description.

a. _____each member has name on roster.

b. _____members do not know who belongs.

c. _____membership decided by God from eternity.

d. _____contains unbelievers (hypocrites).

e. _____members joined when baptized.

f. _____owns property and has a name.

g. _____led by a pastor, minister, or priest.

h. _____will end on Judgment Day.

i. _____Christ is the real leader.

j. _____sometimes makes mistakes.

4. Talk about these questions with your classmates.

God has called you out to be a part of His church. You are special and important. You are a member of Christ's body.

a. How do you feel, knowing this?

b. What do you do as part of Christ's body?

c. How would you like to feel, knowing that God called you out to be part of His church?

d. What would you like to do as a member of the community of "called-out ones"?

God placed all things under His [Christ's] feet and appointed Him to be head over everything for the church, which is His body, the fullness of Him who fills everything in every way.

Ephesians 1:22-23

SESSION 2

God Makes It Work

STRETCHING

From the assignments in session 1, what did you discover about your entrance into the church? Anything interesting? If so, share some of these stories with the members of your class. You might discover some familiar names as you hear each other's stories.

You are discovering what God's actions look like from our side of eternity. Of course, we'd like to see the whole master plan from God's side. But that will have to wait.

Today we will look at how God begins and sustains the church—as we see it from our side. Paul's letter to the Colossian Christians helps us to see this.

GETTING THE WORD:
Colossians 1:1-2

Compare this greeting with that of yesterday's session, **Ephesians 1:1-2.** What is the same? What is different?

_____

_____

Paul wrote this letter around A.D. 60 while in prison in Rome. Even though he had never met these people personally, he felt a need to help them by writing this letter. This need was presented by Epaphras, a Christian from Colossae. He had come to Rome to ask Paul for some help in stamping out some false teaching.

Paul begins his response by showing how God establishes His church through the efforts of people.

Verses 3-8

1. Can you detect from this section the way the Gospel is spread? Of course, the *Gospel* (the Good News of salvation) begins with Christ Himself. Read His command to His disciples in **Matthew 28:16-20.** Which words in **Colossians 1:5-6** show that the disciples did what Jesus commanded?

_____

2. Someone brought the Gospel to these people.

Who was it?

_____

3. The next step shows that the Gospel brings out good results where it is preached. What words does Paul use in **verse 6** to tell that this has happened?

_____

Finally, the Colossian congregation was to share the Good News with others. This entire procedure can be diagrammed in this way:

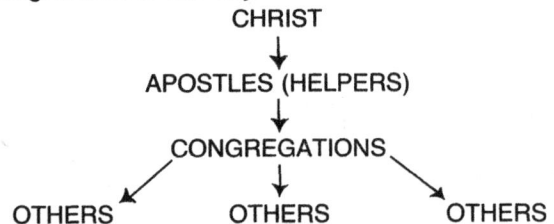

CHRIST
↓
APOSTLES (HELPERS)
↓
CONGREGATIONS
↙   ↓   ↘
OTHERS   OTHERS   OTHERS

Verse 9

According to this verse, Christian leaders spend much time praying for their people.

1. What did Jesus pray for on behalf of His disciples in **John 17:6-25?**

_____

2. What did Paul pray for on behalf of the Christians at Philippi **(Philippians 1:3-11)?**

_____

3. What should we pray for?

_____

Verses 10-12

1. Each member of the church has a unique way of spreading the Good News. Most of us do it simply by the way we live our lives. Individually and collectively as the church we show that the Spirit is working in us. What, according to **verse 10,** is the real reason why Christians **"live a life worthy of the Lord"?**

_____

2. List the verbs and participles in these verses that show the Christian witness.

_____

_____

Verses 13-14

Here is the "bottom line" reason for God to establish His church. Here is the reason for the witness that the church gives to the world. Here is the reason why you are a part of it. State this reason in your own words.

_____

_____

_____

PRACTICE

1. Using the ideas from **verses 3-8,** trace the path the Gospel has taken to get to you. If you come from a family that has been Christian for many generations, this path might resemble a family tree. If the Gospel came to you through a friend or through your school or church, you might think of yourself as a branch grafted into *their* family tree. Let your teacher help you through the early Christian era and the Middle Ages. You might need the entire chalkboard to do this.

2. In **verse 10** we read of **bearing fruit.** Paul used this same picture when he wrote about **the fruit of the Spirit** in **Galatians 5:22-23.** We can think of fruit as the signs in our lives that God's Spirit is producing good things through us. After each fruit in the list that follows, write the name of someone you know who provides a good example of that characteristic. (You may name the same person more than once.)

love _____

joy _____

peace _____

patience _____

kindness _____

goodness _____

faithfulness _____

gentleness _____

self-control _____

Perhaps you named some person that others in the class don't know or think of. Why not share with them in this? Who knows, maybe you are on someone's list.

3. You read what Jesus and Paul prayed for. To help you get started in praying for each other, write your name on a small piece of paper. List one or two real spiritual needs that you have. (If you wish, use the fruit of the Spirit list above to help you get started.) Exchange your list with someone in your class. Remember this person's needs in your prayers. After one week, talk with your prayer partner to discuss your needs and how God answered them.

4. Read **verses 13-14** again. Does this sound like a rescue from a dungeon? Write a paragraph or two describing the dungeon from which Christ has rescued you. (Since you are writing something very personal, write your paragraphs on a separate sheet of paper.)

If this rescue has not happened yet, write what it is that you need to be rescued from. You may or may not wish to share this with the class.

He has rescued us from the dominion of darkness and brought us into the kingdom of the Son He loves, in whom we have redemption, the forgiveness of sins.

Colossians 1:13-14

SESSION 3

God's Miracle

STRETCHING

Do you recycle bottles, cans, and newspapers? Lots of people today are into recycling—especially older people who must live on a fixed income. Besides providing them with a small extra income, recycling gives them something to do.

One of these people is Herb, Tony's neighbor. Many mornings Tony sees Herb loading bottles and cans into the trunk of his car.

One Saturday Tony was taking care of Donny, his 6-year-old cousin. Donny wanted some ice cream, so Tony walked with him to the local ice-cream store. Suddenly, from out of the dumpster in back of the store, Herb appeared, holding a boxful of bottles.

"Hi, there, Tony!" called Herb. "Have a good day."

"Hi, Herb!" returned Tony. "You too."

That night when Donny told his parents about things that had happened that day, he began, "Did you know that Tony's friend Herb lives in the dumpster behind the ice-cream store?"

That's how it looked to Donny. It would really seem weird to us, though, if someone lived in a dumpster. But our God not only came to live in a dumpster called earth, he actually recycled what He found there—us. Read on in Paul's letter to the Ephesians and discover what God really did.

GETTING THE WORD
Ephesians 2:1-3

Rather than calling it a garbage dump, Paul refers to our natural state as being more like a graveyard. **"You were dead in your transgressions and sins" (verse 1).**

1. It's hard to visualize that we can be alive physically and yet be dead spiritually. In **verse 3,** Paul lists the spiritual foul odors given off by those who are spiritually dead. Give examples of them from life today and tell where they can be found.

_____

_____

2. Also in **verse 3,** Paul states who the spiritually dead are. Who are **the rest** and who are **we?**

_____

_____

3. According to this, all people at one time or another were spiritually dead. When were you "spiritually dead"?

_____

Verses 4-10

1. As we have noted before, who does all the acting? Give examples.

_____

_____

2. Particularly note **verses 8-9.** This is one of the great gems of the Gospel. Describe what heaven would be like if each person got there by being good.

_____

_____

3. Read **verses 4, 6,** and **10** again. What miracles of God are reported here?

_____

_____

Our conversion then is entirely a miracle of God. Just as Adam could not "help" God create him, and just as a dead person cannot "help" in being resurrected **(verses 4-6),** so we do not "help" or "assist" God in our conversion.

Verses 11-18

Here Paul refers to the great **wall of hostility** between Jew and Gentile. The Jews hated the Gentiles (non-Jews) and even called them **dogs (Mark 7:27-28).** The Gentiles looked down on the Jews as being "out of step," "aloof," and "narrow-minded."

1. In **verse 17** who are **"you who were far away"? "those who were near"?**

_____

_____

2. What is it that has brought both groups together, making them spiritually alive **(verse 13)?**

_____

3. Referring back to **verses 8-9,** what can Jew and Gentile brag about in regard to their salvation?

_____

4. God's miracle, then, is making both Jew and Gentile spiritually alive. When did this happen in your life?

_____

According to this section, our salvation does not depend on our remembering, feeling, or even experiencing our conversion. It rests solely on God's miracle of making us alive in Christ.

PRACTICE

1. We all know about creatures that live in a sewer or garbage dump. Our world today also contains lots of people who enjoy living in the spiritual sewer or, as Paul says, **transgressions and sins.**

Form groups of 2 or 3 students to examine a recent issue of a newspaper or magazine. Circle stories, ads, or features that are based on people living in sin and enjoying it. Share your findings with the class. Post some on the board under the title "Life in the Sewer."

2. Using the same newspapers and magazines, look for stories, ads, and features based on a fruit of the Spirit (session 2, **Galatians 5:22-23**). Circle them. Share those also with the class. Post them under "Life in the Light." Of which kind are there more? Why is this so?

3. Did you enjoy looking for "Life in the Sewer" items more than you did those of "Life in the Light"? If so, does this mean that God has not "resurrected" you?

Read **Romans 7:14-25** together. What is it that causes you to enjoy reading and thinking about "Life in the Sewer?" How often does this warfare occur in your life? When will you be free from this conflict? _Talk about it._

4. Look again at **Ephesians 2:10.** "Workmanship" denotes great care and skill on the part of the Workman, God. "Created" means "made from nothing" (in our case less than nothing, our old sinful nature). God created this "workmanship" so we can imitate Him in doing good things. How good an imitator are you? As your teacher reads the beginnings of 10 sentences, complete them with the first thought that comes to mind.

If Jesus were in your class today and He would have to choose the following, He would . . .

a. _____

b. _____

c. _____

d. _____

e. _____

f. _____

g. _____

h. _____

i. _____

j. _____

It is by grace you have been saved, through faith—and this is not from yourselves, it is the gift of God—not by works, so that no one can boast. For we are God's workmanship, created in Christ Jesus to do good works, which God prepared in advance for us to do.

Ephesians 2:8-10

SESSION 4
God's Building Project

STRETCHING

During the 2½ years Paul spent in Ephesus, he became well acquainted with the Temple of Artemis (Diana; now in ruins and hardly able to be seen), one of the Seven Wonders of the World. It was four times the size of the more famous Parthenon in Athens. You will learn more about it in session 24.

Paul may have been thinking of this magnificent structure when he wrote the picture of the church found in *Ephesians 2:19-22.* Before we study Paul's picture, let us look at how ancient temples were built.

We need to guess at much of what the ancient builders did. For example, the foundation stones were quarried and brought to the building site from many miles away. These huge stones weighed many tons apiece and had to be dragged over rugged terrain. But each one fit exactly next to the others and didn't need any reinforcing rods or concrete to secure them. Some fit so tightly together that not even a piece of paper could slip between them.

The most important foundation stone was called the cornerstone. Besides being at a corner, it was the stone from which all measurements were taken. Sight lines and angles (vertical and horizontal) were all reckoned from this stone. For that reason, it had to be perfect, strong, durable, not easily damaged. It was part of the foundation and was the only stone that determined measurements for the structure itself.

As the above facts suggest, a cornerstone was a *very* critical part of an ancient building. Mere gravity was the only glue that kept the columns, lintels, and cornices in place. One errant measurement or angle taken from the cornerstone would cause the structure to come crashing down.

The rest of the temple was also composed of stone work—including columns, lintels, cornices, and capitals. Many of these stones were carved into various works of art. Master craftsmen would sculpt these chosen stones into beautiful figures that would fit exactly into the overall scheme. No wonder it took years—even many generations in some cases—to build some of these temples!

Think of these facts as you read **Ephesians 2:19-22.** Then answer the questions that follow.

GETTING THE WORD
Ephesians 2:19-22

1. When Paul wrote, "**You are no longer foreigners and aliens,**" he was referring to the _____

_____.

2. The phrase, "**God's people and members of God's household,**" refers to the _____.

3. The above facts suggest the following message from Paul in **verse 19:**

_____

_____

4. In God's church, what are the foundation stones?

_____

5. This (4) refers to God's Word in the Old and the New Testaments. From the description in "**Stretching,**" point out two similarities between God's Word and ancient temple foundation stones.

   a. _____

   b. _____

6. Using the same comparison, point out three similarities between Jesus Christ and the cornerstone.

a. _____

b. _____

c. _____

7. Use the above information to explain **verse 21.**

_____

_____

_____

8. How can God live in and through each Christian and yet, according to **verse 22,** dwell within this spiritual temple?

_____

_____

9. Now read **1 Peter 2:4-10.** What does God expect of you as a part of His temple **(verse 5)?**

_____

_____

10. Which two verses of **1 Peter 2:4-10** repeat Paul's message in **Ephesians 2:14-18?** _____

_____

11. **1 Peter 2:7b** refers to **Psalm 118:22.** The builders who rejected the stone were the Jewish church leadership. How was this prophecy fulfilled in the life of Christ?

_____

_____

PRACTICE

When Paul wrote, **"You too are being built together"** (Ephesians 2:22), he implied that God is placing you into His church to be used to His glory. Think of yourself now as a stone that God wished to place into His building. Answer the following questions as honestly as you can. No one will read the answers unless you want them to. (If you prefer, write your answers on a separate sheet of paper.)

1. How do you rate your strength spiritually?

a. I give in to pressure from stones around me.

b. I hold my own.

c. I exert pressure on other stones to see things my way.

d. Other.

2. What do you know of your hidden cracks or defects?

a. I am shot through with serious cracks.

b. I have a few dings, but nothing serious.

c. I, as far as I know, have no cracks or defects.

d. Other.

3. At this point in your life as a stone, how much chiseling and shaping has God done?

a. I am just as God found me—no changes.

b. God has given me a few well-placed chops; has taken off rough edges.

c. God has almost completely rearranged me; I bear little resemblance to the former me.

d. Other.

4. Where in the building would you like to be placed?

a. Right up front where I can be seen.

b. Someplace where I won't be noticed.

c. I don't care—up front or out back is OK.

d. Other.

5. Which function in the building would you like to fill?

a. A weight-bearer—holding up other stones.

b. Strictly ornamental; to bring pleasure to others.

c. At a point of heavy wear, where lots of action takes place.

d. Other.

WRAP-UP

Read **Psalm 122** together with your fellow "stones." As you read, think of yourself as a part of the house of the Lord.

You are no longer foreigners and aliens, but fellow citizens with God's people and members of God's household, built on the foundation of the apostles and prophets, with Christ Jesus Himself as the chief cornerstone.

Ephesians 2:19-20

SESSION 5

God's Collection of Gifts

STRETCHING

Some people are givers, and others are takers. A giver is like a dear uncle who had something in his pocket for you every time he came to visit—candy, a toy, or something else that made you happy. When Christmas or your birthday came, your uncle's present was the best, because he knew what you liked.

A taker is like someone—maybe your dad's cousin—who would bring you a present at Christmas or on your birthday, but his presents weren't any fun. And then when he came to visit, he would insist that you sit by him and talk, and so he took away your playtime.

In the church, God is a giver. More precisely, God the Holy Spirit is the Giver. He not only makes you feel good, He also gives you and your fellow believers the spiritual gifts you need. In today's lesson you will examine the gifts the Holy Spirit gives to the church and how they are to be used.

GETTING THE WORD
1 Corinthians 12:1-3

Here Paul writes about *spiritual gifts.* These three verses show what's necessary before we can receive the gifts mentioned later in the chapter. We must say (and believe) that **Jesus is Lord.**

For some of us this happened when we were baptized as infants. Others of us came to faith in Jesus as Savior later in life. For all of us—those who believed as infants and those who came to faith in Jesus later in life—who is it that really caused this to happen?

_____

_____

Verses 4-11

1. Besides creating faith in our hearts, the Holy Spirit gives to the church those who perform acts of service **(verse 5).** These gifts come through the efforts of many different kinds of people. We often call them "spiritual gifts." According to **verse 7,** what is the purpose of all these gifts?

_____

2. Look at the list of gifts in **verses 8-10.** On a separate sheet of paper give an example of someone who received and used these gifts "then" and "now" (in Paul's time and today). Be ready to tell how each person used the gift within the church for the common good. Note that God may not give all these gifts to His church today.

   a. message of wisdom **(verse 8)**
   b. message of knowledge **(verse 8)**
   c. faith **(verse 9)**
   d. healing **(verse 9)**
   e. miraculous powers **(verse 10)**
   f. prophecy **(verse 10)**
   g. ability to distinguish between spirits **(verse 10)**
   h. ability to speak in different kinds of tongues **(verse 10)**
   i. interpretation of tongues **(verse 10)**

3. Note that Paul repeats in **verse 11** that **all these are the work of one and the same Spirit.** Apparently the Corinthians had trouble with tensions in their church, and Paul wanted them to know that, in spite of great diversity, all these gifts were for the benefit of the church. According to **Ephesians 4:15-16,** what benefit is common to all of these gifts?

_____

_____

Verses 12-27

To show the Corinthians how foolish it was to become jealous of one another, Paul constructed this wonderful analogy. It shows how the church is like a human body. Read this section and visualize what Paul is writing. In 10 words or less, tell what these words say to *us.*

_____

_____

Verses 28-31

After you read these verses, compare them with **verses 8-10.**

1. What similarities do you find?

_____

_____

2. What differences?

_____

_____

3. Explain how these words serve as a climax to the entire chapter.

_____

_____

Ephesians 4:14-16

In these verses Paul again used the analogy of the church being the body of Christ. Here, however, Paul gives more specific instructions about how to eliminate the problem of body parts that get in the way of each other.

1. What is one of the signs that body parts are not functioning properly **(verse 14)?** What does Paul call such people? Why?

_____

2. When body parts (members) are in confusion, how will they become organized again **(verse 15)?**

_____

3. Describe how this can happen in the church **(verse 16).**

_____

_____

4. How can love **(verse 16)** cause all the members to function in harmony? Give some examples.

_____

_____

PRACTICE

1. Recall what you read in **1 Corinthians 12:12-27.** Then get ready to roleplay. Pretend that the various parts of the body can talk. They are arguing about who is most important. What would they say?

The eye versus the ear
The foot versus the hand
The heart versus the brain

The lungs versus the stomach

2. Now pretend that one of the parts of the body is unhappy. What would that part say, and how would the other parts of the body respond?

a. The nose complains of mistreatment. The ears, hair, and mouth try to console it.

b. The foot would like to be able to see. What would the eyes and ears say?

c. The stomach says it has been given a bad reputation. It lists all of the terrrible things it will do if the situation is not corrected. Other parts respond.

3. Complete the directions given in one of the following paragraphs. Follow your teacher's instructions.

a. Write a paragraph describing a time when you were sick or injured. In the second paragraph compare this to how the church sometimes acts when there is jealousy or disagreement. In the third paragraph express your opinion on how church members can put aside their differences and become unified in Christ.

b. Write a paragraph describing the problems within the membership of an athletic team. In the second paragraph compare this to the way a body malfunctions. In paragraph three, suggest what can be done to solve the team problem. (Don't rely on merely saying, "They shouldn't . . . " Be positive—show how a living faith in Christ can solve the problems.)

c. We often conclude our solutions to spiritual problems by saying, "Let Jesus solve it" or "If you take your problem to Jesus, He will take care of it." In this paragraph or two, be specific. How does Jesus solve our disagreements? How does Jesus take care of our problems? (Do not rule out the possibility that Jesus may not solve our problems exactly as we would.)

d. Write a solution to this problem. *The members of the church youth fellowship are choosing up sides. One of their members, Marcie, seems to assume that she has the right to decide what the group will do. After all, her father is the president of the congregation, and when the group chooses her ideas, they seem to get more support from adults in the congregation. Other members think Marcie is stuck-up and always gets her way. They say that if Marcie keeps getting her way, they will leave.*

Speaking the truth in love, we will in all things grow up into Him who is the Head, that is, Christ. From Him the whole body, joined and held together by every supporting ligament, grows and builds itself up in love, as each part does its work.

Ephesians 4:15-16

UNIT 2:

How the Church Lives

Track and field isn't exactly a team sport. Even though points are tallied and team victories are recorded, those who compete might be more interested in doing their personal bests and breaking individual records.

Team sports weren't very common in the apostle Paul's time. Paul's reference to the church as Christ's body and to us as its members must have sounded revolutionary to his readers!

Paul would probably be very interested in the team sports that we enjoy today! He'd approve of team spirit and cooperation. He'd cheer individual participants and give praise to players, coaches, and teams. He'd love game strategy where each team member has a function to fulfill and a goal to achieve. But, for Paul and for us, the greatest joy is always in whom we serve—our Lord Jesus Christ.

Think of the many pieces of athletic equipment a track-and-field team needs—batons, stopwatches, hurdles, starting blocks, poles, and more. As we, who are the church, learn how we can better serve our Lord and Savior, we discover a remarkable fact: Our Lord Jesus has provided us with *everything* that we need as a team!

The theme in this unit is "togetherness." You'll discover how much we need each other, how God provides for our needs, what He has for us to do, and how He helps us pull and work on His team.

If you're a member of an athletic team, your coaches have probably talked to your team very many times! You might have experienced this as a member of a different team, too—a debate team, a journalism team, a scholastic quiz team, and other kinds of teams at school. Remember the spirited remarks your coaches made after a victory? Remember the quiet, consoling words after a loss or a failure? Remember the stern tongue-lashings at halftime or during practice when the team wasn't performing well?

Through these talks, the coaches compliment, console, encourage, and correct each team member, doing so *as a part of your team and for the good of the team!* Through the writings of Paul in this unit, God will do the same with us. But you will notice that the way in which He does it goes beyond what any coach can do: He gave His Son's life for us so that we can be on His team!

And now God gives us the power
to *be* His team,
to *live* as His team members,
to *practice* together in Christian teamwork,
to *grow* in Christian fellowship and faith,
and to *celebrate the victory* that Jesus has won for us!

SESSION 6
Sticking Together

STRETCHING

In unit 1 we looked at the body as a picture Paul used for the church. Paul often used analogies and comparisons to illustrate his theological message.

Your teacher will list 10 physical items that Paul used to describe the following. See if you can match them.

1. The Holy Spirit _____

2. Good works _____

3. Satan's kingdom _____

4. Our former life under Satan _____

5. The Law with commandments and regulations

_____

6. The Old and New Testaments _____

7. Jesus Christ _____

8. Believers _____

9. The church _____

10. Those who work in the church _____

How many did you get right? More than half? You must be in tune with Paul's method of teaching.

In this session we will look at Paul's purpose for using such teaching devices. His words in **Romans 1:8-17** point out what Jesus wants us to do for each other.

GETTING THE WORD

This letter is similar to the letter to the Colossians in that Paul had never been to either city. Nevertheless, he counted these Christians as his friends and promised that soon he would come to see them.

Romans 1:8-10

1. Why does Paul thank God for the Roman Christians?

_____

2. What may have been the signs of their faith **reported all over the world?**

_____

Verses 11-13

1. Why does Paul want to visit these people?

_____

2. What spiritual gifts would strengthen them? (Look back to **1 Corinthians 12.**)

_____

3. Now find out what Paul actually did when he lived in Rome **(Acts 28:30-31).** Who in your life does this for you?

_____

4. Paul would also benefit from the faith and witness of the Roman Christians. When and how are you able to strengthen the faith of your fellow believers? Give examples. Consider the following settings:

Your home

Your school

Your team

Your congregation

5. When Paul speaks of a harvest in **verse 13**, what is he referring to?

Verses 14-15

1. What nationalities were represented in the Roman congregation?

_____

2. How is it possible for various races, economic levels, and backgrounds to make up a unified church?

_____

_____

Verses 16-17

In these two verses Paul provides a theme that continues throughout the book. These words also reflect Paul's guiding philosophy as he did his mission work.

1. In Paul's day Rome was the center of power and prestige. Every kind of new philosophy or religion could be found there. Nevertheless, what does Paul say about the Gospel?

_____

2. What is there about the simple Gospel that might sound stupid to the world?

_____

3. To Paul, the Gospel was "the power of God for salvation." The Greek word for power is *dynamis*—our *dynamite*. How is the Gospel like dynamite?

4. God reveals His righteousness in the Gospel. This would ordinarily cause us to feel uncomfortable. It need not, though, since we sinners are considered holy because God sees us in the light of His holiness. According to **verse 17**, and **Romans 3:22**, how are we sinners turned into "righteous people"?

_____

_____

5. How, then, can you help a fellow believer feel good about himself or herself?

_____

_____

PRACTICE

Form groups of two or three persons. Talk about your likes, dislikes, fears, and hopes with each other. If you have trouble getting started, try some of these topics.

1. I thought I was a goner one time when . . .

2. I like to daydream about . . .

3. My mom and dad think I am good at . . .

4. Fifteen years from now I'll be . . .

5. I really felt proud when . . .

After each member of the group has had a chance to speak and answer questions, write a short note to each member of your group. Write each note on a separate sheet of paper. Compliment the person on a quality revealed in the sharing time. One good way to begin is to write: "I really appreciate the way you . . . ."

Be truthful and positive. Then exchange the notes with each other. Notice how you feel. Notice the expressions on the faces of your classmates. This is what happens when we share the Gospel with one another.

I long to see you so that I may impart to you some spiritual gift to make you strong—that is, that you and I may be mutually encouraged by each other's faith.

Romans 1:11-12

SESSION 7

Listening Together

STRETCHING

Where do you eat lunch at school? Before schools had cafeterias and snack bars, students usually brought their lunches in brown bags or black lunch boxes.

Pretend that some famous people from the Bible carried their lunches with them. Try to identify each person by the lunch. Here are nine lunches. Who are the owners?

1. Five rolls and two fish
2. Consecrated bread from the tabernacle
3. Honey from the carcass of a lion
4. Vegetables and water
5. A loaf of bread and a jar of water
6. Curds, milk, and roasted calf
7. Thin flakes of bread that taste like wafers made with honey
8. A scroll
9. Lentil stew

This little quiz is not intended to make you hungry. Rather, it should help you think about the kind of food on which the church lives. The church is the body of Christ. To remain strong, this body must eat. Read St. Paul's message to his young friend, Timothy, on this subject in **1 Timothy 4:1-15.**

GETTING THE WORD

Answer the questions in this section on another sheet of paper.

1 Timothy 4:1-5

Paul begins by reminding Timothy of agents of Satan who will come into the church and try to peddle spiritual junk food.

1. Give some examples of junk food that you eat. Why do people call it junk food?

2. To what junk-food teachings does Paul refer in these verses? These heresies (false teachings) were apparently popular in Paul's time. What false teachings are being spread today?

Verses 6-8

Here Paul refers to being **"brought up in the truths of the faith and of the good teaching that you have followed."** These truths are what Jesus taught.

1. Look up **Mark 7:18-19.** What did Jesus have to say about which foods are clean? Paul repeats this message in **1 Timothy 4:4.**

2. What does the church need to identify to combat false doctrine?

Verses 9-11

1. According to **verses 9-10,** what is the most important truth on which our entire spiritual life is based?

2. Very simply, what are we to do with this truth **(verse 11)?**

Verses 12-16

Perhaps Timothy was only in his very early 20s. Paul urges him to combat others' criticism of his youth by setting a good example **(verse 12).**

1. What does Paul want Timothy to do in **verse 13?**

2. What activities of the church today fulfill this command?

3. When is this done publicly? When is it done privately?

4. Paul expected Timothy to progress in his ministry **(verse 15).** What personal skills will improve as *you* know more of God's Word?

5. Which congregational skills will improve as the "called-out ones" learn more of God's Word?

6. Discuss this with your classmates: Does the church today preach and teach God's Word enough?

PRACTICE

1. Were you first exposed to God's Word when you were a little child? If so, you may be able to fill in all the blanks that follow. If you first heard God's Word later in life, fill in only the blanks that apply to you.

a. The first prayer you learned

_____

_____

b. Who taught you this prayer?

_____

c. The first church you remember attending

_____

d. The name of your first Sunday-school or day-school teacher

_____

e. The pastor who confirmed you

_____

f. The color of the cover of your first Bible

_____

g. Not counting this class, the last place where you heard God's Word

_____

2. As a class, think of all the ways God's Word can be transmitted. Have someone write them on the board. Here are some starters: *Your mouth, writing, photocopy machine*

_____

_____

3. As individuals, we hear God's Word in everyday life. We also hear it in our local congregation when it is preached and taught. List various parts of a Sunday morning service. Tell how God's Word is presented in those parts. Two examples are given.

a. Hymns—texts are based on Scripture passages

b. The bulletin or program—contains Bible references

c. _____

d. _____

e. _____

f. _____

4. Recall the activity in session 2 where you were asked to pray for the spiritual needs of a friend for one week. Get together with this friend and see what has happened.

Perhaps, at the end of your visit with your friend, you could pray for each other.

In connection with this activity, recall that God's Word tells us to pray for each other **(Ephesians 6:18)**.

Until I come, devote yourself to the public reading of Scripture, to preaching and to teaching.
1 Timothy 4:13

SESSION 8

Receiving Together

STRETCHING

James' grandfather had died. Since the funeral was held in a faraway state, James did not attend. His mother had gone and now was back. She told James that before Grandfather died, he had written James a letter and had wanted him to have two items.

As James read the short letter, cherished memories of Grandfather crossed his mind and tears welled in his eyes.

Then Mother brought out two small packages. The first was in a torn and crumpled envelope. Inside was a strange-looking legal document with faded wording and signatures. Mother said it had belonged to James' great-grandfather who had, in his younger years, been a slave. This document said that James' great-grandfather had been freed by his owner. Grandfather had written that he wanted James to have it so that he would never forget his ancestors.

The second item was a carefully carved figure of a proud stallion pawing the air. James' grandfather had been an expert woodcarver, and this was one of his most admired works. He had written, "I want you to have this so that you will not forget me, nor lose sight of what you can become."

All three objects became cherished possessions for James. The letter was his grandfather's last message to him, the document reminded him where he came from, and the stallion reminded him of his grandfather who loved him, and of what that love could become in him.

GETTING THE WORD

Understanding Baptism and Holy Communion

The preceding story is an analogy picturing the two sacraments of the church. A sacrament is an act of God through which He gives His undeserved kindness to His church in a special way. God gave us two sacraments, Holy Baptism and Holy Communion. Read **Matthew 28:16-20** and **1 Corinthians 11:23-26** to find out how Jesus Christ instituted (began) them.

Both sacraments are based on God's Word and require us to believe what He says. In both, God commands us to use physical substances that involve our senses. He gave both to believers to forgive our sins and strengthen our faith.

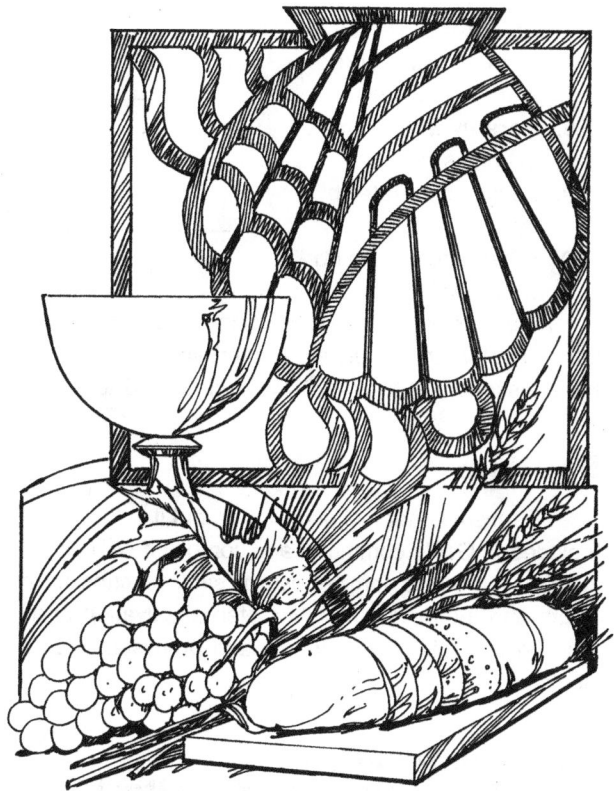

In Holy Baptism we use Jesus' words plus water. Through Baptism God washes away our sins and brings us into His family.

In Holy Communion we use Jesus' words plus bread and wine. Jesus told us that the bread and wine we eat and drink are really Himself. We really do receive His true body and blood in, with, and under the bread and wine. Through Communion God forgives our sins and strengthens our faith.

Thoroughly discuss these sacraments and their meaning with your teacher. Then fill out the chart below to compare the sacraments with the story under **"Stretching."**

	The Story	The Church
1. The gifts	_____	_____
2. The giver of gifts	_____	_____
3. The reason for gifts	_____	_____
4. The receiver	_____	_____
5. Object that explains significance of gifts	_____	_____
6. Object that remembers giver; gives hope to receiver	_____	_____
7. Object that remembers giver; gives hope to receiver	_____	_____
8. Person who transmits gifts	_____	_____
9. Feeling generated by gifts	_____	_____
10. What receiver will do with gifts	_____	_____

Below are two explanations of the sacraments written by Dr. Martin Luther. After you read them, discuss the questions that follow with your class and teacher.

Baptism

"Baptism is not just plain water, but it is the water included in God's command and combined with God's word. . . . It works forgiveness of sins, rescues from death and the devil, and gives eternal salvation to all who believe this, as the words and promises of God declare."

Holy Communion
(The Sacrament of the Altar)

"[The Sacrament of the Altar] is the true body and blood of our Lord Jesus Christ under the bread and wine, instituted by Christ Himself for us Christians to eat and to drink. . . . These words, **Given and shed for you for the forgiveness of sins,** show us that in the Sacrament forgiveness of sins, life, and salvation are given us through these words. For where there is forgiveness of sins, there is also life and salvation."

Some Questions About Baptism and Holy Communion

1. Even though a person is baptized only once, how can he or she make daily use of Baptism?

2. If a person is baptized and then loses faith in Christ as Savior, will that person go to heaven? Defend your answer.

3. Read **Matthew 28:16-20** again. Why can infants be baptized also?

4. How do we know that Jesus' true body and blood are really present in the Sacrament?

5. How often should a "called-out one" partake of the Sacrament? Why?

6. Could a person commune too often? Why or why not?

PRACTICE

1. These questions may have raised others in your mind. Write yours on a piece of paper without attaching your name. Turn them in for discussion and answers.

2. If time allows, talk about Baptism and Holy Communion practices carried on in congregations with which you are acquainted. How much variety in practice do you think God allows?

Repent and be baptized, everyone of you, in the name of Jesus Christ for the forgiveness of your sins.

Acts 2:38

Whenever you eat this bread and drink this cup, you proclaim the Lord's death until He comes.

1 Corinthians 11:26

SESSION 9

Working Together

STRETCHING

Let's review what the church is and what it does. This will prepare us for a look at how the church works together.

Complete these statements. If you need help, look at the titles and main points of sessions 1—8.

1. God created the _____

2. God makes it work by means of the _____

_____

3. God's miracle is _____

4. God's building project is _____

5. God's collection of gifts is _____

6. The church sticks together when _____

_____

_____

7. The church listens together to_____

_____

8. The church receives God's grace through

_____

_____

_____ , and _____

The eight topics already covered would not be complete if this were all of the story. God has done so many things for the church. Now He calls on us to do something. Let us see what this is.

GETTING THE WORD

God gave His first work assignment to Jesus Christ. Jesus knew very well what His work would be. On more than one occasion he told His hearers what it was.

1. Read **John 3:16-18.** What was Jesus' main mission?

_____

2. To make this understandable to people, what

did Jesus do for three years during his public ministry **(Luke 7:22-23)**?

_____

_____

3. In doing this, Jesus also fulfilled what the Old Testament said about Him. Read **Luke 4:18-20.** Write the Old Testament reference which Jesus quotes about Himself.

_____

_____

Of course, Jesus had to do this work alone, especially the assignment of **John 3:16.**

4. What did Jesus command His disciples to do in **Matthew 28:19**?

_____

5. In **Acts 1:8** Jesus used the term **witnesses** to describe what His disciples would be. What does a witness do?

_____

_____

6. As the "called-out ones," we, too, are Jesus' witnesses. What will a good witness do?

_____

What will an ineffective witness do?

_____

7. In **2 Corinthians 5:18,** what does Paul call this work?

_____

8. In **2 Corinthians 5:20** Paul gives us the title of *ambassador.* What does an ambassador do?

_____

9. Putting these two answers together, we can be called Jesus' ambassadors of reconciliation. Can an ambassador of reconciliation fulfill Jesus' assignment

with or without other ambassadors? _____
Tell why or why not.

_____

It is clear, therefore, that God calls each individual

member to be a witness, wherever he or she is sent. God also provides support and strength for each individual member through others in the church.

PRACTICE

In session 7 you read some of Paul's words to Timothy, one of his helpers. Another helper, Titus, apparently was an older, more experienced troubleshooter. Read Paul's advice to him in **Titus 2.** This advice to various kinds of people provides advice on how we can be good witnesses of Jesus Christ today.

1. How should older men
a. Handle liquor **(1 Timothy 3:2)?**

_____

b. Gain the respect of their families, fellow workers, employees **(Ephesians 4:32)?**

_____

c. Build up their own faith **(2 Timothy 1:13-14)?**

_____

d. Control their temper **(Ephesians 4:26)?**

_____

2. How should older women
a. Handle conversations over the phone **(Ephesians 4:25)?**

_____

b. Treat their husbands **(Ephesians 5:22)?**

_____

c. Raise their children **(Ephesians 6:4)?**

_____

3. How should young men
a. Learn self-control **(1 Thessalonians 4:3-7)?**

_____

b. Practice integrity **(2 Corinthians 5:14)?**

_____

c. Exhibit a godly tongue **(James 3:9-12)?**

_____

4. How should employees
a. React to their employers **(Ephesians 6:5-8)?**

_____

b. Talk about their employers **(1 Peter 2:13-17)?**

_____

c. Gain the trust of others **(Colossians 3:12-14)?**

_____

The grace of God that brings salvation has appeared to all men. It teaches us to say "No" to ungodliness and worldly passions, and to live self-controlled, upright and godly lives in this present age.

Titus 2:11-12

SESSION 10

Concluding Activities for Units 1–2

Answer the following questions. They will help you review the first two units. Write your answers on a separate sheet of paper.

TERMS

Write a short definition for each of the following terms:

1. Ambassador
2. Cornerstone
3. Create
4. Ecclesia
5. Grace
6. Heresy
7. Reconcile
8. Sacrament
9. Saints
10. Witness
11. Baptism
12. Body of Christ
13. Christ
14. Church
15. Colossian Christians
16. Epaphras
17. Ephesus
18. Fruit of the Spirit
19. Gifts of the Spirit
20. Gospel
21. Holy Communion
22. Jesus
23. Paul
24. Roman Christians
25. Titus

SHORT ANSWER

1. In **Ephesians 1:3-14** Paul mentions seven actions that God does for the "called-out ones." What are they? How do those actions affect you?

2. What are some differences between the invisible church (the "community of called-out ones") and the visible church (congregation, organization, or denomination)?

3. Review **Colossians 1:10-14.** How does God bring the Gospel to people today?

4. Review **Ephesians 2:1-18.** How much of the credit for your conversion should you receive? How much credit should go to God?

5. Review **Ephesians 2:19-22.** Which parts of this analogy are most helpful for you in understanding God's church?

6. What insights do you get about the church from the analogy of the human body?

7. Review **Romans 1:11-13.** When has someone encouraged you in a way similar to the way Paul encouraged the Romans? When have you encouraged someone else this way?

8. Review **1 Timothy 4.** List instructions you think Paul would give to the church today.

9. Review **Matthew 28:16-20** and **1 Corinthians 11:23-26.** In 15 words or less, state the main things a Christian should know about Baptism. Do the same for Holy Communion.

10. Review **John 3:16-18.** Write a short letter to someone who doesn't believe in Jesus for salvation. Tell him or her about the hope you have.

11. Review **Galatians 5:22-23.** Which fruit of the Spirit do you see most among your classmates? Which fruit do you wish *you* would have in greater abundance? Why?

12. Review **1 Corinthians 12.** How does God use the gifts of the Spirit in the church today?

UNIT 3:

Worship, the Church's Breath

Whether you call them wind sprints, running the lines, or interval training, they are all the same—hard work! Getting in shape is hard work and there is no easy way to do it.

All those conditioning workouts are designed to improve your cardiovascular system. As you get in shape, your body makes more efficient use of the oxygen you inhale. That means that you breathe more deeply and your heart does not beat as fast. When in shape, your body is a wonderfully efficient organism.

God is also concerned that we as members of the church are in shape—spiritually. The workout that the church does is called worship. In this unit we will see how the Holy Spirit breathes into us the Word of God and how we exhale our acts of love and devotion. As we grow in faith, our breathing becomes more efficient, our worship more meaningful.

In this unit also you will worship with your classmates. This will be more than the usual prayer and Bible reading. You will actually have an opportunity to practice your spiritual breathing by planning and celebrating through worship.

To prepare for this, you will learn about elements of worship that St. Paul describes. You also have an opportunity to evaluate the various acts of worship that the church now practices.

And you thought church was a place to go and sit for an hour and listen to someone talk! You thought that it was a place where you couldn't talk! You thought going to church was boring! It's as boring as a scrimmage; as uninteresting as seeing last week's game film; as unexciting as winning first place in the 4 x 100 relay!

SESSION 11

Centering Worship

STRETCHING

Look at this picture. You can find a scene like this almost any summer evening in almost any neighborhood. Yet, if someone were to suggest that these people were worshiping, you might think that they were looking at a different picture than you were.

But it is true. These people are all worshiping. One simple definition of worship is "doing any activity that demonstrates or acknowledges the worth of someone or something."

Take, for example, the man washing his car. His worship shows that he values his car and wants to preserve its beauty. Look at the other people in the picture. What are they worshiping? What are they doing in order to worship?

Think of your life. What do you consider really worthwhile? What do you do to demonstrate that worth? Of all the items you have mentioned, which is the most important to you?

For a "called-out one," the most important Being is God. God created you, redeemed you through Christ, and now promises you everlasting life. Therefore He should be the center of your life.

This was also true in Old Testament days. God saved the children of Israel, just as He saves us. Then He taught them how He was to be the center of their worship. But what happened? In our Bible reading today we will see how they turned to other things and worshiped them.

GETTING THE WORD
1 Corinthians 10: 1-5

Do you recall the incidents Paul was writing about? To refresh your memory, read about some of them. Look up these references and be ready to summarize the event.

"Under the cloud . . . they all passed through the sea" (Exodus 13:20-22; 14:19-31).

"They all ate the same spiritual food and drank the same spiritual drink" (Exodus 15:22-27; 16:13-36).

1. In what ways was Israel's crossing the Red Sea similar to your baptism? How do these incidents establish God as Number One with them and with you?

2. What similarities can you find between the manna eaten by Israel and Holy Communion eaten and drunk by you? How do these incidents further establish God as Number One?

3. How can these incidents lead a "called-out one" to worship to "thank for something" rather than to "get something"?

Verses 6-10

Here Paul tells how Israel replaced God with something else as the center of their worship. Read each reference. Then answer these questions for each incident:

a. What replaced God as Number One? Why?

b. What actions became worship by this replacement?

1. "Do not be idolators, as some of them were." **Exodus 32:1-6**

   a. _____

   b. _____

2. "We should not commit sexual immorality, as some of them did." **Numbers 25.**

   a. _____

   b. _____

3. "We should not test the Lord, as some of them did." **Numbers 21:4-9**

a. _____

b. _____

4. "Do not grumble, as some of them did." **Numbers 16:41-50**

a. _____

b. _____

Verses 11-13

In these verses Paul applies Israel's lessons to the Corinthians—and to us.

1. According to **verse 12,** what is a sure way to fall into false worship? What do those who think they stand firm look like?

_____

_____

2. What good news does Paul give in **verse 13?**

_____

_____

3. What is "the way out" of temptation? Perhaps you and others in your class can give some examples of how this has happened. Share them with one another.

PRACTICE

1. Sometimes the same activity can be either worship of God or worship of a replacement for God. Homework, for example, can become worship of God when we do it honestly, at the right time, and to the best of our ability. It can become worship of self when we use someone else's answers or write down anything just to "get done."

How can we worship God through each of the following activities? How could the same activity become worship of a replacement?

a. Going to church

Worship of God _____

Worship of a replacement _____

b. Giving an offering at chapel

Worship of God _____

Worship of a replacement _____

c. Writing a letter to a friend

Worship of God _____

Worship of a replacement _____

d. Singing a solo in church

Worship of God _____

Worship of a replacement _____

e. Praying

Worship of God _____

Worship of a replacement _____

f. Spiking the ball

Worship of God _____

Worship of a replacement _____

g. Listening to a sermon in church

Worship of God _____

Worship of a replacement _____

2. Pretend that this happened to you: During a math test the person in front of you has inadvertently left the formulas for the equations out where you can see them. You could tell the person to put them away, but then you may get into trouble for talking. You could say nothing, but then your teacher may accuse you of cheating. You recall that God has promised not to let you be tempted beyond what you can handle. What will you do? Write your answer in a paragraph and be ready to read it tomorrow.

These things occurred as examples to keep us from setting our hearts on evil things as they did.
1 Corinthians 10:6

SESSION 12

Sharing Worship

STRETCHING

Some years ago near a Midwestern farming community there lived a well-to-do farmer named Luke. Luke had always been an active member of the local congregation. But lately the pastor had seen less and less of Luke on Sundays.

One day the pastor met Luke at the general store. "Say, Luke," began the pastor, "I haven't seen you at church lately. Where've you been?"

"Oh," replied Luke, "I don't have time. Besides, I can read my Bible and say my prayers at home."

With that Luke headed out the door, leaving the pastor with his next statement still unsaid.

Some months went by. Still Luke failed to appear in church on Sundays. Finally, on a cold, rainy day the pastor hitched up his team and drove out to Luke's farm. Luke met him at the door and silently led him into the parlor. He motioned for his pastor to have a seat in front of the fireplace. Both of the men sat silently, staring into the fire; both were trying to think of how to say just the right thing.

Quietly, the pastor rose, went to the fire, lifted out one bright coal with the tongs, and set it on the hearth. As the pastor sat back in his chair, both men gazed at the coal, which gradually turned dark as it cooled. Just as it was about to flicker out, the pastor rose, picked it up with the tongs, and placed it back into the fire. Before he even sat down again, the coal suddenly burst back into flames.

"All right, Pastor," said Luke, "you made your point. I'll be back next Sunday."

And he was.

What message did Luke get?

GETTING THE WORD

Whatever the message that Luke received, he learned the difference between private and corporate worship. Private worship is intensely personal, may have no set form, and satisfies the needs of an individual believer to express a personal relationship with God.

But as we have seen, an individual needs to worship with other "called-out ones." What happens when individuals with various, differing needs and practices get together to worship? What will the group do? Read **1 Corinthians 14:26-33** to learn what happened in the worship services at Corinth.

1. Describe what a Corinthian worship service may have been like.

_____

_____

_____

2. Why was there apparently no order to their meetings?

_____

_____

_____

3. What would be the result of such a worship service?

_____

_____

_____

4. Whose preferences would most likely be agreed to? Why?

_____

_____

_____

We use **corporate worship** as a name for what happens when "called-out ones" gather together to worship. Corporate comes from the word *corpus,* which means *body.* How does this term fit with Paul's picture of the church? Reread **1 Corinthians 14:26-33** and look for Paul's solution to the problem in that congregation.

5. What is the underlying reason for any act of corporate worship?

_____

_____

6. Why should one who speaks in tongues keep

quiet if there is no interpreter?

_____

_____

7. Who should be given priority in speaking?

_____

_____

8. What is Paul's final reason for doing things in an orderly manner?

_____

_____

PRACTICE

1. We still hear Luke's reasons for staying away from corporate worship. How would you answer the following excuses?

a. "I watch services on TV. I hear better sermons, the choirs are better, and I don't have to leave home."

b. "I can worship better out in the woods. In the quiet I can see God's handiwork in nature. I don't have to put up with the hypocrites at church."

c. "People make me nervous. I don't like crowds, crying babies, and being crowded on an uncomfortable bench."

d. "They just want my money. I'd rather write a check from home to a charity I choose. They waste a lot of money anyway."

2. Moving from private worship to corporate worship makes some demands on the worshiper. Read **Acts 4:32-35.** Why were all the believers **one in heart and mind?** How would this same feeling apply to corporate worship?

_____

_____

3. Assume that you and 11 others are planning a worship service. List a corporate worship activity that will accomplish the same purposes as the private worship activity in the first column.

Private	Corporate
Asking God to forgive you.	_____
Listening to a tape of a Christian rock group.	_____
Reading from a devotion book.	_____
Thinking about whether God still loves you.	_____

4. Recalling the flickering coal that burned brightly after being put back in the fire:

—Write what benefit each of the following is to an individual "called-out one."

—Decide if this benefit could occur if the "called-out one" was worshiping alone.

	Benefit	Yes or No
Congregational singing	_____	_____
Hearing the Gospel read	_____	_____
Saying the Apostles' Creed	_____	_____
Saying the Confession of Sins	_____	_____
Going to Communion	_____	_____
Praying for congregation members	_____	_____
Shaking hands with the pastor	_____	_____
Seeing 85-year-old Grandma Smith go to Communion	_____	_____
Seeing 1-month-old Michelle Renée Brown baptized	_____	_____

Let the word of Christ dwell in you richly as you teach and admonish one another with all wisdom, and as you sing psalms, hymns and spiritual songs with gratitude in your hearts to God.

Colossians 3:16

SESSION 13

Receiving in Worship

STRETCHING

One of the most obvious signs of life is breathing. **Genesis 2:7** records man's first breath: God **"breathed into his [man's] nostrils the breath of life, and the man became a living being."**

Just so we in the church receive breath. That breath of life comes from the Holy Spirit. As the church lives, works, and grows, it breathes—inhaling and exhaling. We can think of the breath the church **inhales** as the grace of God: all the blessings God gives through His Word.

We use the term *sacramental* to describe the acts in corporate worship when we inhale God's grace. Such action by God results in gifts to His church to give life, just as oxygen gives life to living organisms.

In this session we will examine these sacramental gifts of God. In the next session we will study those activities that are like **exhaling**. We call these the sacrificial acts—acts through which we show God our love and devotion.

GETTING THE WORD
Form in Worship

The church has worshiped in many different ways. God does not dictate what form the church must use in worship. Jesus once told the woman of Samaria, **"God is spirit, and His worshipers must worship in spirit and in truth" (John 4:24).** God requires only that whatever we do as worship should truthfully demonstrate the love and respect we have in our hearts.

Worship has, therefore, taken many forms and undergone many changes down through the years. Today many Lutheran, Roman Catholic, and Episcopal churches use a *liturgical* style of worship. A liturgical style follows a set outline that does not vary. Within that outline, however, are parts that change from week to week. This style guarantees a set framework for worshipers. They know they will experience a balance of sacramental and sacrificial acts. Effective use of a liturgical style also provides enough variety to insure a fresh look at God's story of salvation each week.

The roots of liturgical worship extend back to the Jewish synagogue worship of the intertestamental period. As the centuries passed, both good and bad changes occurred. During the Middle Ages, the basic service was called the Mass, a shortened version of the phrase "You are dismissed," spoken by the priest at the end of the service.

During the Reformation period Martin Luther retained the Mass, eliminating only the parts that were contrary to Scripture. He also provided more opportunity for the worshipers to become more actively involved, mainly through singing.

Liturgical churches today still use the Mass, but with many variations. For our discussion we will use the divine service as used in the Lutheran church. No matter which hymnal you use, the basic parts are the same.

Sacramental Acts of Worship

Three basic activities that occur in each service can be labeled sacramental. In each God gives us a fresh breath of His divine grace. All three repeat the story of salvation, with Christ the center of all action.

1. **The absolution: God forgives our sins.** Read

31

1 Timothy 1:12-17. As we approach God, we are aware, as was Paul, of our massive record of sins **(verses 13 and 16)**. Along with Paul, God pours out His grace abundantly, forgiving our sins. He does this only through Christ, who **"came into the world to save sinners."**

Before we can come into God's presence, the problem of sin must be settled. We cannot do this by excusing ourselves, blaming others, or ignoring it. No, the only way to handle sin is to throw ourselves completely on the mercy of God, believing Jesus' words, **"Son, [daughter,] your sins are forgiven" (Mark 2:5).**

Find the words of absolution in the service you use in your church.

2. **The lessons: God gives us His Word.** Read **2 Timothy 3:14-17**. Having been made right with God, and now eager to learn from Him of the vast treasures of His grace, we listen to Him speak. Paul tells Timothy that **"the holy Scriptures . . . are able to make you wise for salvation."** Scripture does this by **"teaching, rebuking, correcting, and training in righteousness."** The eventual outcome is that God will have trained you to be **"thoroughly equipped for every good work."**

This usually happens in a service through three readings (Old Testament, Epistle, Gospel) and a sermon. The readings proclaim the lesson directly from God's Word. The sermon explains and applies this Word to the church's life.

3. **The Sacraments: God gives us Himself in Holy Communion and Holy Baptism.** Read **Matthew 26:26-28** and **Acts 2:38-39**. As we saw in session 8, both sacraments give us the forgiveness of sins in a concrete, personal way. A service reaches its climax as the "called-out ones" approach the One who calls, forgives, and assures. As each communicant receives Christ's body and blood, he or she comes as close to Jesus Christ as is possible this side of heaven. What a gift! What a way to leave God's special presence!

PRACTICE

Give brief but complete answers to the following questions. Have them ready for discussion and correction at the beginning of session 14.

1. Explain the analogy that compares breathing and worship.

2. Define *sacramental, sacrificial,* and *liturgical.*

3. What requirement for our worship did Jesus give?

4. Why are there so many ways to worship?

5. What are some advantages of liturgical worship?

6. How did the service receive the name "Mass"?

7. What use did Martin Luther make of the Mass?

8. What are the three sacramental activities in liturgical worship?

9. Why must we settle the matter of sin before we can continue our worship?

10. What is the purpose of hearing God's Word in the service?

11. Why is Holy Communion the closest we can come to our Savior in this life?

12. Why should Holy Baptism normally be performed during the service?

I rejoiced with those who said to me, "Let us go to the house of the Lord."

Psalm 122:1

SESSION 14

Giving in Worship

STRETCHING

As an introduction to this session and as a review of the last one, talk about the answers you wrote for the questions in session 13. You will again see how, in the sacramental acts of worship, the church receives God's grace.

You noticed that a person who can only inhale will soon die. That will also happen to the church if it *only receives* God's grace. Without sharing or giving it away, the church soon would become self-centered and spiritually dead. Therefore liturgical worship also includes sacrificial elements, times when the church gives back to God its acts of love and devotion. You will look at these sacrificial acts in this session.

GETTING THE WORD

Sacrificial Worship

1. The term *sacrificial* comes from the Old Testament act of worship, the sacrifice. The sacrifice was an object that was worth much to the worshipers. They sacrificed grain, cattle, bread, and produce.They would then voluntarily give this item to the Lord, normally receiving nothing from the gift for themselves. The usual method of sacrifice was burning. As the item was consumed in the flame, the worshipers could visualize God accepting it. In summary:
   —The gift had worth.
   —It would be given voluntarily.
   —The worshiper normally would get nothing in return.
2. We can, therefore, see the following criteria for sacrificial acts of worship:
   —The act results from God's grace to us. We don't give in order to receive; rather, we receive and then react by giving.
   —The act is a voluntary action from us to God. When we are motivated and perform an act for any reason other than because we love God or others, we are not performing a sacrificial act of worship. We do, of course, often derive many blessings from our giving, but they should never be the reason for giving.

—The act is always directed to God or to others, who may represent God to us.

3. Sacrificial acts of worship can be divided into three categories: songs, prayers, and offerings. In all these acts the gathered "called-out ones" unite to offer their individual gifts as one. In so uniting voices, thoughts, and objects, God confirms and strengthens each individual's faith. This point is important: *God does not need our gifts, but we need to give them.* We need to exhale God's grace as a part of our spiritual life.

What Does God Say?

1. The following Scripture references describe types of sacrifices in our worship. Read each reference and write the words that verify the criterion from 2 above.
Songs: Colossians 3:15-17
   a. result of grace

   _____

   b. voluntary

   _____

   c. to God/others

   _____

Prayers: 1 Timothy 2:1-8
   a. result of grace

   _____

   b. voluntary

   _____

   c. to God/others

   _____

Offerings: 2 Corinthians 8:1-7
   a. result of grace

   _____

   b. voluntary

   _____

   c. to God/others

   _____

PRACTICE

1. These three acts take many forms in a worship service. Following are the titles of some of these acts. For each act answer the three questions that follow (on another sheet of paper).

    Introit
    Kyrie
    Hymn of Praise
    Sermon Hymn
    Offertory
    Offering
    Prayers
    Agnus Dei
    Post-Communion Hymn

a. From which of God's gifts is it a result?
b. To whom is it directed?
c. Is it primarily a song, prayer, or offering?

2. Some parts of the service have been retained by tradition or introduced by common usage. In order for them to be valid acts of worship they should be sacramental or sacrificial. Below is a partial list of these. Under the leadership of your instructor, decide the following:

a. Is it sacramental or sacrificial?
b. If sacramental, what is the grace God gives? If sacrificial, to whom is it directed? as a result of what?
c. Does it edify the church?

    Organ prelude
    Announcements
    Apostles' or Nicene Creed
    Pax
    Salutation
    Children's sermon
    Introduction of visitors
    Choir anthem
    Benediction
    Applause

Guard your steps when you go to the house of God. Go near to listen rather than to offer the sacrifice of fools, who do not know that they do wrong.
Ecclesiastes 5:1

SESSION 15

Worshiping

STRETCHING

After four sessions learning about Christian worship, take time now to *do* worship. During this session your class will worship together as the church.

By this time you should be organized and ready to worship together. Whether you choose to use a form of worship from your hymnal or to devise your own, the following rules (called rubrics) can help make your worship meaningful and reverent.

1. Offer silence as your first gift to the Lord. It is a simple but obvious sign that you and your fellow worshipers are ready to put yourselves at God's disposal.

2. Stand when praying, speaking, singing liturgical responses, or as a sign of respect (for example, while singing a hymn stanza that praises the Triune God). We often stand for the reading of a particular portion of Scripture, especially for the Gospel.

3. Sit for hymns and when being instructed (for example, during the Old Testament and Epistle readings and during the sermon).

4. Kneel when confessing your sins. Many Christians also kneel while praying some of the great prayers of the church, such as the Litany and the Bidding Prayer.

5. Offer silent prayers before and after the service. Before the service ask God to help you participate meaningfully. After the service thank God for the opportunity to worship and ask Him to cause the Word you have heard to bring forth fruit in your life.

May the Holy Spirit direct your thoughts and guide your actions during this special time.

GETTING THE WORD

The service itself will provide God's Word for this session. You will find the Word in the various readings, sermon, hymns, and liturgy. Don't let this become a mere exercise. Rather, allow the Lord to speak to you through your classmates.

PRACTICE

After you conclude the worship, talk about the following questions.

1. Describe the area in which you worshiped. How did it help or hinder meaningful worship?

2. How was music used?

3. Which of the sacramental acts were most meaningful to you? Why?

4. At which point did worshiping with others seem most uplifting?

5. Which sacrificial act did you feel most enthusiastic about? Why?

6. What suggestions can you make for the next time your class worships together?

Sing to the Lord a new song;
sing to the Lord, all the earth.
Sing to the Lord, praise His name;
proclaim His salvation day after day.
Declare His glory among the nations,
His marvelous deeds among all peoples.
Psalm 96:1-3

UNIT 4:

Growth, the Church's Life

Everyone remembers physical fitness tests—the chin-ups, the push-ups, the sit-ups, and the running. They are exhausting, but in a way they are fun. You find out how you compare with other students your age. But more important to you and to your instructor, you also find out whether you have improved. The only way to find out is to test.

The church also needs to improve in the way it lives as the body of Christ. But we have no simple "spiritual fitness tests" to check on improvement. Only God knows exactly how the church is doing. Yet, as members of the church, we should be concerned about our spiritual growth.

St. Paul was also concerned about his garden of congregations. He once said, **"I planted the seed, Appollos watered it, but God made it grow" (1 Corinthians 3:6).** He understood that where spiritual growth occurs, it is God who causes it.

In this unit you will continue your study of the church by seeing how it grows within a local congregation. You will also begin to find out about your own congregation and how God made it grow. Perhaps a pastor from a nearby congregation will share with you the joys of caring for God's people and helping them to grow.

Continuing the analogy of plants and growth, one must also include something about garden pests. Yes, even in the church we find diseases and insects that would slow or even stop growth. We want to know about these also.

What a wonderful feeling to finish a quarter-mile time trial in less than your old time! What a satisfied feeling to eat the first ear of corn from the garden you planted! And what a pleasure it must be for our Lord to look at you and see steady spiritual growth! How it must please Him to see a group of believers work together to make His kingdom bigger and better!

What is true about plants is also true of people. If you grow, you're alive; if you don't, you're dead!

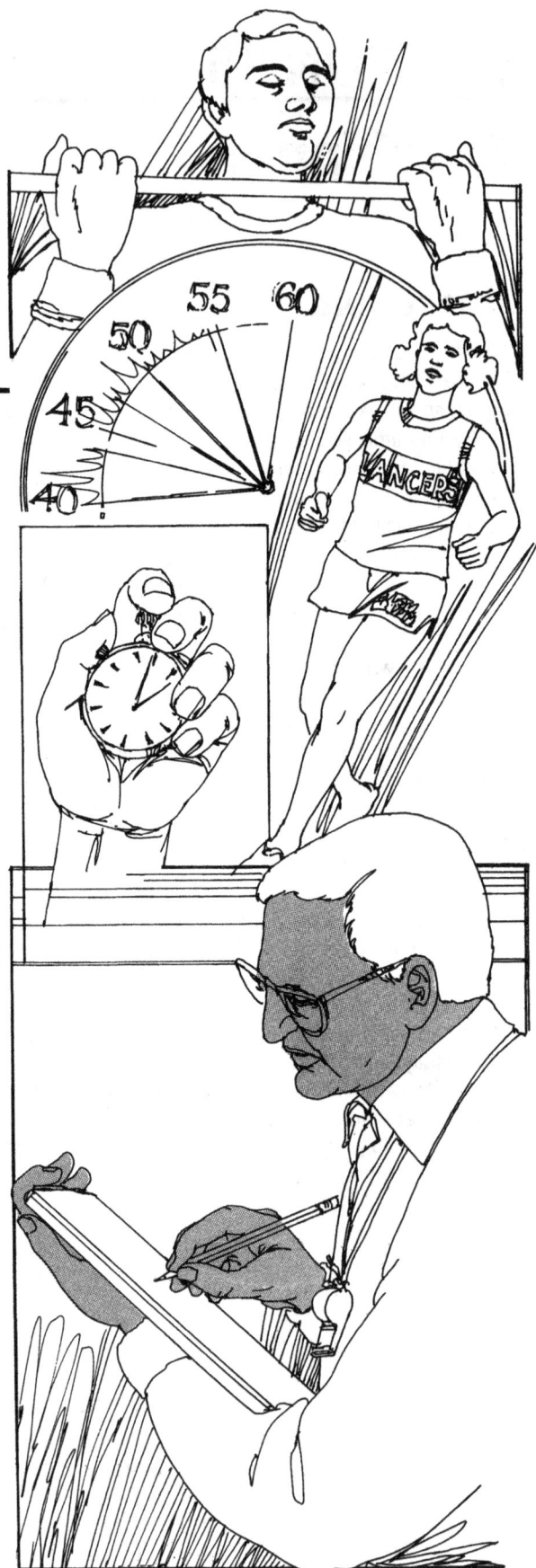

SESSION 16

Planting the Seed

STRETCHING

Growth. God causes many kinds of growth. Complete this puzzle about one thing He causes to grow—plants.

Across

1. **Matthew 6:28-30;** here today, gone tomorrow
4. **Luke 8:11;** the seed is the _____
5. **Exodus 15:27;** place of 70 palm trees
8. **1 Corinthians 3:6;** _____ watered Paul's seeds
10. **Luke 13:6-7;** tree having no fruit
11. **John 15:1-8;** Jesus is the true _____
12. **Matthew 13:24-30;** what an enemy planted (singular)

Down

2. **Luke 11:42;** Pharisee counted out 1/10 of these
3. **Isaiah 55:10;** rain results in _____ for us to eat
4. **Matthew 6:28-34;** these will not produce clothes

6. **Matthew 6:28-29;** these are dressed better than Solomon
7. **Matthew 13:31-32;** small seeds that yield a large plant
9. **Romans 11:13-21;** tree to which Gentiles are grafted

Growth in a plant is one sign of life. Similarly, growth in the church is a sure sign that the Holy Spirit is active. In today's session you will look at how the church begins its growth.

GETTING THE WORD

Have you ever observed the beginning of a congregation? One forms when a group of "called-out ones" gathers together to affirm and exercise their faith. This section tell of one such congregation. It consisted of three members.

1. Read 2 **Timothy 1:3-12.** Who were they, and why is this a congregation?

_____

_____

The home is the first and most basic gathering of "called-out ones." When similar families gather together, they form a local congregation, and a need for spiritual leadership arises.

2. Who was chosen to be such at leader in **2 Timothy 1:6?** _____ in

1:11? _____

3. The "called-out ones" gathered together because of the Gospel. Summarize the Gospel message Paul gives in **1:9-10.**

_____

_____

_____

4. We can use the following formula to show how a "gathering of called-out ones" may begin:

The Gospel + One Who Speaks It + Hearers + Holy Spirit = Gathering of Called-out Ones

Each of the following references describes the formation of such a gathering. For each, tell:

a. Clear Gospel quote
b. Speaker
c. Hearers
d. Evidence of Holy Spirit
e. Name of congregation

John 20:19-23

a. _____

b. _____

c. _____

d. _____

e. _____

Acts 2:14-41

a. _____

b. _____

c. _____

d. _____

e. _____

Acts 10:24-48

a. _____

b. _____

c. _____

d. _____

e. _____

Acts 19:1-7

a. _____

b. _____

c. _____

d. _____

e. _____

5. Returning to the idea of plant growth, compare the beginning of a "gathering of called-out ones" with seed germination.

Elements Necessary for Seeds to Germinate	Formula for Church Germination
Seed	_____
Farmer	_____
Soil	_____
Heat and moisture	_____
Germination	_____

PRACTICE

In previous sessions we used the term *church* for the entire community of "called-out ones." Now we will begin using a term for the local gathering of "called-out ones." We will refer to this group as the "congregation."

Beginning with **"Practice"** in this session, you will be asked to find out facts about the formation of your congregation. Today find answers to the following:

1. Who was the first individual to proclaim the Gospel to your congregation?

2. Where was the first service held?

3. When did this take place?

4. What were the reasons this congregation was started?

5. What are some of the interesting facts about its beginning? (For example: difficulties and surprising blessings)

6. Who were some of the first members?

In the next three sessions you will be asked to find more information about your congregation. Start now to make contacts to find out this information. Your pastor, congregational president, church secretary, or director of Christian education may be able to help you. Ask to see anniversary books, old bulletins, newspaper clippings, and names of older members who might have more information.

They devoted themselves to the apostles' teaching and to the fellowship, to the breaking of bread and to prayer. . . . And the Lord added to their number daily those who were being saved.

Acts 2:42, 47b

SESSION 17

Nurturing the Crop

STRETCHING

Think again about a group of families who have established a congregation. What should be its purpose?

Consider each of the following organizations. Decide which has purposes closest to those of a congregation.

1. *A country club:* Members pay to join; receive many benefits (golf, swimming, tennis, food, social life); can decide who may join and who may not.

2. *A corporation:* Controlled by a board of directors; organized to make a profit; manufactures product or provides a service; successful when profits exceed expenses.

3. *A government:* Run by elected officials who obey a constitution; organized to keep order and provide certain services for citizens; must defend territory when invaded.

4. *A school:* Governed by a board; organized to educate students for useful life; administered by principal and teachers.

As you discuss these organizations, you will, no doubt, discover some ways each of the four organizations is similar to a congregation. To help you decide which has the most similar purposes, read **2 Timothy 2:1-10.**

GETTING THE WORD

Notice that Paul again begins with God's grace. We bring nothing to our salvation; God brings everything.

2 Timothy 2:1-2

1. How can a person and a congregation be **"strong in the grace that is in Christ Jesus"?**

_____

_____

2. What should Timothy entrust to qualified men to be taught to others?

_____

_____

3. What, therefore, is a prime purpose of a congregation?

_____

_____

Verses 3-7

At times the task of proclaiming the Gospel seems hard or dangerous. When we don't get the response we expect from others in the congregation, the task becomes frustrating. As Paul discusses these facts, he uses examples of three types of workers.

1. *The soldier:* What soldier hardships are similar to hardships of Gospel teachers? Who is the "commanding officer" whom the congregation tries to please?

_____

_____

_____

2. *The athlete:* What rules must an athlete follow in order to be successful? What are some rules that our "Coach" has laid out for us to follow? (See also **verses 15-16** and **1 John 4:7-12.**)

_____

_____

_____

_____

3. *The farmer:* What are the "crops" from which the congregation should receive a share? (Remember the analogy of seed and growth.)

_____

_____

_____

Verses 8-10

1. Notice how Paul repeats again his motivation: **"Jesus Christ, raised from the dead."** He also refers again to the hardships laid on him, **"being chained**

like a criminal." After saying this, Paul states his goal. What is it?

_____

_____

2. What, therefore, is the goal of the congregation as it proclaims the Gospel?

_____

3. Which of the four organizations in **"Stretching"** comes the closest to a congregation? Why?

_____

_____

PRACTICE

1. Your instructor may have invited a pastor from a local congregation to visit your class. He will tell you of the life of a minister of the Gospel. Listen especially to the list of opportunities he has to proclaim the Word. Be prepared to ask questions about his work and its effect.

Write a summary of his presentation.

Name of pastor _____

Name of congregation _____

Number of years in the ministry _____

Summary of presentation: _____

_____

_____

_____

_____

2. Referring again to **"Stretching"**, write your ideas of what a congregation would be like if its goals were the same as:

a. A country club: to have fun

_____

_____

b. A corporation: to make a profit

_____

_____

c. A government: to keep the peace

_____

_____

d. A school: to educate

_____

_____

3. Continue with your report from session 16. Find information to answer these questions.

a. Who is your present pastor? What is his background and training?

b. How many adult and teenage Bible classes are held weekly? What is the average attendance in each per week?

c. How does your congregation proclaim the Gospel to the community?

d. Write a quote or two from your pastor about the goals he sees for your congregation.

The things you have heard me say in the presence of many witnesses entrust to reliable men who will also be qualified to teach others.

2 Timothy 2:2

SESSION 18

Guarding Against Pests

STRETCHING

In the last session we discovered that proclaiming the Gospel in a congregation can be difficult and dangerous. In this session we will find out why. Returning to the analogy of a congregation being like a plant, let us look at the enemies of plants.

Enemies of plants fall into four classes: disease, insect, animal, and human. Disease, animal, and insect enemies are quite obvious as they either chew or disable a plant into death. Humans, however, often have good intentions but no knowledge when they kill plants. Or we think we can improve our own lives if we cut them down, pull them up, or plow them under. Whether caused by bacteria, bug, or bulldozer, dead plants are dead.

Let us return to **2 Timothy** to hear St. Paul warn his young friend, Timothy, against the enemies of the church. As we read, let us think in terms of all three kinds of garden pests.

GETTING THE WORD
2 Timothy 2:14-19

These verses speak of diseases that cause great damage to a congregation.

1. **Word Blight (verse 14)** causes members to argue unnecessarily about the meanings of words. Members become angry at each other; many lose their love and drop out.

2. **Word Chatter (verse 16)** causes members to expend too much energy in meetings, lectures, and discussions on topics that have nothing to do with the Gospel. They become so busy talking that they don't have time to hear the Gospel. This disease spreads quickly because it looks like everyone is busy, but no solid nurture results.

3. **God's Cure (verses 15 and 19):** To combat both diseases, St. Paul prescribes that members learn how to handle the Word. That way is to acknowledge that it is the Lord who saves (**"the Lord knows those who are His"**) and to **"turn away from wickedness."** The wickedness he refers to here is that of nurturing

sinful pride by trying to win stupid arguments and by trying to talk one's way into eternity.

2 Timothy 2:22-26

This section speaks of "spiritual insects."

1. **Young Stem Sucker (verse 22)** attacks especially young members. It sucks out of them their faith, love, and peace and replaces these with evil desires. These are especially the desires of youth for pleasure in drugs, alcohol, sex, and excitement. Victims drop out of congregational life, since they don't find these pleasures there.

2. **Winged Quarrel Starter (verses 23 and 25)** will attack members who may have been weakened by Word Blight and Word Chatter. This insect lays eggs that look like innocent differences of opinion. But when they hatch, they turn into large-scale arguments about insignificant issues. Members end up arguing for their pride rather than for the Gospel of Christ.

3. **God's Repellent (verses 20-22):** The people used water to clean their articles, the same water that cleans us so we become useful for God. Baptism is God's water of cleansing. Remembering your Baptism is an excellent way of beginning each day. As Martin Luther says, "the old Adam in us should by daily contrition and repentance be drowned and die with all sins and evil desires, and . . . a new man should daily emerge and arise to live before God in righteousness and purity forever."

2 Timothy 3:1—4:5

The greatest danger to the congregational plant, however, comes from would-be leaders and those whose influence affects the members.

1. **The Good-Looking Gardening Company (3:1-9).** Paul diagnoses the danger from this group in **verse 5: "having a form of godliness but denying its power."** Using a disguise of pseudo love, sincerity, and smooth talk, they come up empty because they are not motivated by the power of God, the Gospel of Jesus Christ. You can follow their trail of destruction in **verses**

2-4 and in **6-8.** But to those members who can see clearly, their true identity will be discovered.

2. **The Foolish Fertilizer Company (4:3-4).** This is, perhaps, the most dangerous of fake gardeners. It pretends to feed the members, but only gives what *sounds* good. Its message sounds so pleasant, so up-beat, that members develop "itching ears"—ears that want more, while souls starve for the real food of the Gospel.

3. **God's Real Care Company (3:10-17; 4:1-2 and 5).** Paul describes the real food of the Gospel in **3:16-17.** It comes from God Himself, since it is God-breathed. It was not invented by someone else. Paul lists its use: **"teaching, rebuking, correcting and training in righteousness."** Plants living on this diet will be **"thoroughly equipped for every good work."**

Paul concludes by telling Timothy to proclaim this Word at all times, in season and out of season. God's plants don't take the winter off; they need constant care and feeding. This, then, is the work of the congregation, to proclaim the Good News and continue to grow from using it.

PRACTICE

1. We have now looked at God's gardening project and the pests that continue to attack it. Now take a look at them in action, and see how God's various remedies fight them.

For each of the pests described, two or three students should take the roles of congregation members who are attacked. They should act out the real-life situations as described. Use your own experiences in congregational life to make each pest and its damage lifelike.

After each pest has been presented, the class should decide how the problem could be solved. Use God's answer as stated by Paul. Agree on practical ways to overcome Satan's work.

If there is time, have the roleplayers reenact their situation. This time use the solution suggested by the class.

2. **Your report:** As the third section in your report, answer these questions:

a. What does your pastor see as large problems in your congregation?

b. What is being done to overcome them?

c. What current false teachings are appearing as problems?

Keep your head in all situations, endure hardship, do the work of an evangelist, discharge all the duties of your ministry.

2 Timothy 4:5

SESSION 19

Measuring Success

STRETCHING

We have been looking at plant life as an example of congregational life. Without looking back, can you match up items from the plant world with those of a congregation?

Plants	Congregation
1. Seed	_____
2. Farmer	_____
3. Soil	_____
4. Heat and moisture	_____
5. Germination	_____
6. Garden pests	_____

Now try to come up with three more comparisons.

7. Flowers	_____
8. Seeds	_____
9. Harvest	_____

We could call these last three items the products of and final purpose of a plant. When a plant produces these three, it has been successful. But what about a congregation? What are the signs of success? Let us return to St. Paul's second letter to Timothy to find out.

GETTING THE WORD
2 Timothy 4:6-8

1. As Paul looked ahead to his own death, he also looked back on his record. Write the three accomplishments he mentioned.

_____

_____

2. Is the **crown of righteousness** Paul mentions in **verse 8** earned or is it a gift? Explain your answer.

_____

3. The three accomplishments Paul lists are actually only one. What is it?

_____

4. Who gets the credit for it? _____

5. Why does the world not count being saved as a success?

_____

_____

_____

_____

Verses 14-18

Besides his personal victory, Paul also mentions another success. Look for it in the questions that follow.

1. What did Alexander try to hinder?

_____

2. Why did the Lord stand at Paul's side and give him strength?

_____

3. Therefore, Paul gave God the credit for giving him what success?

_____

4. From these two examples, we can see that God willed for Paul and for congregations to set two goals. What are they?

PRACTICE

1. Following are some items often considered as evidence of a congregation's success. How can they help or hinder the pursuit of the two success markers listed by Paul: **eternal salvation and proclaiming the Gospel?**

    Large membership
    Beautiful buildings
    Well-known, gifted preacher
    Full calendar (many activities)
    Large budget (big offerings)
    Friendly people
    Professional quality music
    Active youth groups

2. What are some other success markers people today might look for? How does each of these help or hinder the attainment of the primary success marks?

3. Pretend that your congregation has a list of 10 projects it wants to do. Pretend that they all cost about the same. Your task is to put the most urgent at the top of the list and the least urgent at the bottom. Everyone in your group should agree on the exact ranking.

After you finish, write the code word for each project on the proper step below. Here is the list in alphabetical order.

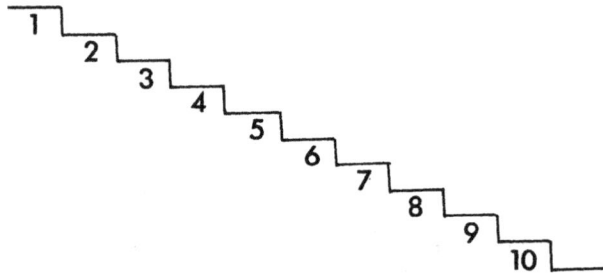

	Code Words
New Bibles and hymnals for the sanctuary	**Bibles**
Redecorate the chancel; install new benches	**Chancel**
Publish a congregation monthly newsletter and a yearly directory in color	**Directory**
Print and distribute a monthly neighborhood evangelism paper	**Evangelism**
Fund a Meals-for-the-Poor program for six months	**Meals**
Sponsor a missionary in a foreign country	**Missionary**
Rebuild and add to the organ	**Organ**
Sponsor a weekly radio evangelism program	**Radio**
Buy a new sound system for youth choir	**Sound**
Buy new uniforms for the church softball and basketball teams	**Uniforms**

4. The final set of questions for your report is on important programs in your congregation.

    a. How does your congregation handle new members?

    b. How is evangelism carried on?

    c. What is your congregation known for in the community?

    d. What improvements would you like to see in your congregation? Why?

The Lord stood at my side and gave me strength, so that through me the message might be fully proclaimed.

2 Timothy 4:17

1
2
3
4
5
6
7
8
9
10

SESSION 20
Concluding Activities for Units 3–4

Take a few minutes to review concepts from units 3 and 4. Both units cover corporate worship, a major activity of the church.

On a separate sheet of paper write one or two sentences about each of the following topics:

1. Why we worship God
2. How we worship God
3. Differences between private and corporate worship
4. Reasons for orderly worship
5. Sacramental acts of worship
6. Sacrificial acts of worship
7. Liturgical worship
8. Three criteria for bringing gifts to the Lord
9. The need to edify during corporate worship
10. Reasons why we stand, sit, or kneel during different parts of a service
11. Three things necessary for a Christian congregation to exist
12. How a congregation is like a plant
13. The prime goal of both pastors and congregations
14. One way a congregation is like a country club, a corporation, a government, and a school
15. Three enemies of the congregation
16. One way to use God's Word against each of these enemies
17. Two goals of a successful congregation
18. Evidence that a congregation is achieving its goals
19. The main reasons *you* attend corporate worship services
20. Three major tasks of someone beginning a new congregation

UNIT 5:

Witnessing, the Church's Work

You know, of course, that your coaches make practice plans. They account for every minute and have a purpose for every activity. These plans are necessary to get the team ready for the real thing—the game.

That is where we are now. We've practiced long enough. It's time for the real thing—Christ's plan for the church's work. And that work is called "witnessing."

To remind us that witnessing is the real activity of the church, the names of the parts of our sessions have changed. Now we will begin with a **"Warm-Up"** and then all participate in **"First Half,"** which is where we will confront the various facets of our task. This will be followed with **"Second Half,"** where we will continue the game plan as it was outlined in **"First Half."**

During these 15 sessions you will receive first-hand tips on how to witness for your Lord from your Lord Himself. St. Paul, one of the greatest witnesses for Christ, will share some of his own history and some insights on how to do it.

Now, don't get the idea that the next session will be on how to ring doorbells or stand on street corners preaching to people. You will see that as one of Jesus' disciples you have spent years witnessing already, and you didn't even know it.

Being a witness is exciting, challenging, and even rewarding. Rewarding? Yes. You already have the reward: salvation. God gave it to you free through Christ. Now He wants you to let people know about it.

That's the game plan. It's time to begin the real work. Now let's see it happen.

SESSION 21

Getting Started

WARM-UP

Have you ever wondered what kind of people God chose to write the books of the Bible? Here is a list of occupations of some Bible writers. Which author goes with which occupation?

1. a doctor _____

2. a winetaster (butler) _____

3. a king _____

4. a priest _____

5. a tentmaker _____

6. a government official _____

7. a shepherd _____

8. a tax collector _____

9. a fisherman _____

10. a soldier _____

Even though these men earned their living in one of these ways, their real business was to witness to the Lord. That is also the business of "the called-out ones"—the church.

In this unit we will follow a very special "called-out one" as he brings his witness to the world. He is St. Paul, God's missionary to the Gentiles. Even though he made tents to keep bread on the table, his real job was giving away the Gospel. His story is really the story of all "called-out ones." It is the story of the church's occupation.

Before you start reading, remember that in Paul's early life as a Christian he still used his Hebrew name, Saul. Later on, during his first missionary journey, he changed it to Paul.

FIRST HALF

Acts 1:8

This short verse contains Jesus' command and plan for the church's task.

1. The power that will move the church to action is the Holy Spirit (God's Breath).

2. **You will be My witnesses.** According to the tense used by Jesus, there is only one choice: What kind of a witness will members of Christ's church be? Whether we are strong or weak witnesses, we *will* witness to our Lord.

3. Notice the three areas Jesus mentions:

a. **in Jerusalem.** The church is to begin its witness right where it is, at home.

b. **and in all Judea and Samaria.** The church is then to move out into the surrounding areas.

c. **and to the ends of the earth.** Finally, the church is to witness to the entire world.

4. Summarize, then, Jesus' plan:

a. Source of power: _____

b. Occupation: _____

c. Order of progression: _____

_____

Acts 9:19b-29

This account follows Saul's conversion on the way to Damascus **(9:1-19a).** It is hard to imagine the tremendous change Saul experienced. The enemy of Christ became His fearless witness. Such is the power of the Holy Spirit. One might think that it would take time for Saul to gather his thoughts, prepare himself, and get acquainted with his new friends in the faith. But such was not the case.

Answer these questions in your own words.

1. When did Saul begin his witness?

_____

2. How can you tell that Saul's witness had a powerful effect on those who heard him?

_____

_____

3. What happened that might have been discouraging to Saul?

_____

_____

4. While he was in Jerusalem, how can you tell that Saul was not discouraged?

_____

_____

5. Why did the "brothers" send Saul home to Tarsus?

_____

_____

6. How did Saul fulfill Christ's command of **Acts 1:8?**

_____

_____

_____

_____

Galatians 1:11-24

In this reading Paul tells how he viewed his conversion. Compare this reading with **Acts 9:19b-29.** Then answer these questions.

1. What seems to be the main point Paul is making in the **Galatians** reading?

_____

_____

2. What point did Luke emphasize in the **Acts** account?

_____

_____

3. How are these emphases similar?

_____

_____

4. According to the **Galatians** reading, where do you think Paul received his vast knowledge of Christianity?

_____

_____

SECOND HALF

1. When the Holy Spirit takes control of an individual, great things begin to happen. We see this in the conversion of Saul. See what else happened to others when God's Spirit took control. Read the following references. Name the person and describe his or her action.
   a. **Numbers 11:24-25**
   b. **Judges 14:5-6**
   c. **1 Samuel 10:9-11**
   d. **Ezekiel 2:1-2; 2:9-3:4**
   e. **Luke 1:67-80**
   f. **Acts 2:1-4**

2. When Jesus said in **Acts 1:8**, "**You will be My witnesses,**" He was naming the main work of the church. The Lord also explained to Ananias in **Acts 9:15** what witnessing is. Copy His words, but insert your name for "this man."

_____

_____

_____

3. Being a witness is not hard, as long as you are truthful. The term "witness" is used most often in a courtroom. There, under oath, a witness merely answers questions asked by court officials.

Your instructor will call some of the class members to the stand. If you are called, merely answer the questions you are asked. As others are being questioned, notice how they answer. Confident, straightforward, factual replies indicate a strong, confident grasp of the facts. This is the kind of witness Christ wants us to be for Him. God can help you be a strong, confident witness for Christ. Just ask Him!

You will receive power when the Holy Spirit comes on you; and you will be My witnesses in Jerusalem, and in all Judea and Samaria, and to the ends of the earth.

Acts 1:8

SESSION 22

Witnessing Where You Are

WARM-UP

Let's play a word-association game. Your teacher will read a word. You are to write down immediately the first word that comes to mind.

1. _____
2. _____
3. _____
4. _____
5. _____
6. _____
7. _____
8. _____

Now look at your list. Your teacher will tell you what your answers mean. You may discover something about how you associate certain words and meanings.

FIRST HALF

The Bait (John 4: 4-15)

When Jesus called Peter and Andrew to be His disciples, He said, **"Come, follow Me, and I will make you fishers of men" (Matthew 4:19).** In this reading from **John** Jesus demonstrates how to do it. When you fish you need bait. In this dialog with the woman of Samaria, Jesus uses bait: a subject that will be of interest to the "fish."

1. What was Jesus' "bait"?

_____

2. Why was this subject of interest to the woman?

_____

3. How did Jesus make this "bait" superattractive to the woman?

_____

_____

4. How do we know that the woman was "interested"?

_____

5. What did Jesus mean by **the water I give him (verse 13)?**

_____

The Hook (verses 16-20)

Bait is useless unless it is attached to a hook. Just so, as we attempt to "catch men," they must be led to feel (sometimes painfully) a need to be caught. This hook is the Law. It exposes their sinfulness and their inability to get free of it by themselves. Notice how Jesus uses this hook.

1. When Jesus told the woman to call her husband, what sin was He exposing?

_____

2. What did Jesus' question reveal to the woman about Himself?

_____

3. Why did the woman change the subject in **verse 20?**

_____

_____

The Line and Pole (verses 21-26)

As the woman flopped about trying to get free of the Law, see how Jesus gently reeled her in. He took what could have become a bitter argument (where to worship) and changed it to an invitation to worship.

1. How did Jesus express this invitation to true worship?

_____

_____

2. How did the woman express her one last attempt at flopping off the hook and line?

_____

_____

3. In so doing she flopped right into Jesus' net. She then came face-to-face with the Divine Fisherman who used a cross-shaped pole. How did Jesus express this?

_____

_____

4. From **verses 27-30** and **39-42** how can you tell that the woman was indeed "caught"?

_____

_____

John does not report that Jesus asked her to believe in Him. Rather, His message was one of pure giving: **"I who speak to you am He" (verse 26).** The fact that later on she said to her townspeople, **"Could this be the Christ?" (verse 29)** shows that God had begun faith within her.

When we witness, Christ merely wants us to present Him and what He has done. He doesn't tell us to create faith. The Holy Spirit does that.

SECOND HALF

1. We could title this part of Jesus' command to His church, **Witness Where You Are.** God has placed us in His mission field. We just need to recognize it. How many people do you come in contact with each day? They are the mission field.

For 24 hours, keep track of the following items. Bring in your record tomorrow to share with the class.

a. Approximate number of people I talked to or who talked to me:

_____

b. Number who expressed unhappiness:

_____

c. Number who expressed joy:

_____

d. Names of three people with whom I talked more than five minutes:

_____

_____

e. Name of person and topic discussed the longest:

_____

f. Names(s) of person(s) who mentioned God in positive way:

_____

g. Name of person who seemed to need the joy of God's peace the most: _____

2. Plan to roleplay a way to do Christian evangelism. While people doing evangelism use many styles and formats, they all try to present a clear statement of the Gospel.

In this roleplaying activity the first person will be the Christian witness. He or she should use Jesus' technique as dictated by the situation and as seen in **John 4.**

Lead up through **"The Bait"** and **"The Hook"** to **"The Line and Pole"** (the clear statement of the Gospel). Do this within a five-minute time limit.

The second person should act out the role dictated by the situation. Give answers as logically and as honestly as the actual person would do it.

Situations:

a. Lunch time at the company cafeteria. The subject has just had a massive argument with the boss. One can detect bitterness, resentment, and even plans for retaliation.

b. Subject has just broken up with boyfriend or girlfriend. Subject did not approve of crowd that friend was hanging around with.

c. Subject has just been told that he or she has AIDS. Subject feels overwhelmed by unspoken accusations of friends, hopelessness of recovery, and prospects of a slow death.

d. Subject has just stunned witness by saying that going to church and being a member of a Christian family have been a drag. As soon as he or she can, subject will give it all up.

We no longer believe just because of what you said; now we have heard for ourselves, and we know that this man really is the Savior of the world.
John 4:42

SESSION 23

Speaking to the Neighborhood

WARM-UP

How did your survey go? Remember, you were keeping a 24-hour record of the people with whom you talked. Share your findings either in a small group or with the whole class.

After hearing the results of the surveys, make some observations. Do this as a group.

1. Generally what kind of mood did others show?

2. What subjects seem to cause the most concern?

3. How can the Gospel of Jesus Christ help those who are in trouble?

Think about the people you named who need God's peace. Look for the right time and place to talk with them.

Sometimes witnessing is more effective when it's done by more than one person. That happens when "called-out ones" move on to the next area in Jesus' plan: the neighborhood. Let's follow St. Paul as he moves out from the company of the disciples into his immediate surroundings.

FIRST HALF

Actually, this section is about all of Jesus' followers in and around Palestine. Paul (Saul, as he was called then) was just one of many involved in witnessing to the neighborhood.

While still in your discussion groups, read each section below. Discuss the questions and decide on answers you all can agree with.

Acts 11:19-21

1. How is this section like a description of a local congregation conducting a neighborhood evangelism program?

2. Compare the message of those witnesses with the messages today's congregations give to their communities.

Verses 22-24

1. How was Barnabas like the pastor of a congregation?

2. What should a pastor be most concerned with: calling on the unchurched or building up the faith of his members?

Verses 25-26

1. Suppose Barnabas and Saul were members of your congregation. Make a list of their activities for one week.

2. Speculate on how and why the disciples got the name "Christians."

Verses 27-30

1. How does a local congregation duplicate the activity described in **verses 29-30?**

2. Should a local congregation participate in charitable activities that are not directed to fellow "called-out ones"? Why or why not?

3. Reread **verses 21, 24, 26b,** and **30.** What same idea is presented in all of them?

_____

_____

4. How can this idea be at the same time an encouragement and an exhortation to the church?

_____

_____

_____

SECOND HALF

The Bible provides many examples of those who witnessed to the neighborhood. Many of these examples occurred at work. This is one of the best times to witness, because conversation can be natural, flowing from whatever situation arises. Match the following references and events.

These are the references:

Genesis 12:4-9	**2 Kings 5:2**
Genesis 40:6-8	**Acts 8:26-40**
Numbers 14:1-9	**Acts 10:23-48**
Judges 6:24-32	**Acts 16:22-34**
1 Samuel 16:23	**Acts 18:1-8**

Match the references with the events as follows:
a. Write the reference.
b. Write the name(s) of the witness(es).

1. as a passenger to a seat partner

a. _____

b. _____

2. while performing music

a. _____

b. _____

3. in prison, cheering up the inmates

a. _____

b. _____

4. a word in confidence to the mistress of the house

a. _____

b. _____

5. singing in prison

a. _____

b. _____

6. improving the neighborhood by removing an insult to God

a. _____

b. _____

7. as a guest in a foreigner's home

a. _____

b. _____

8. moving into a new neighborhood

a. _____

b. _____

9. at work making tents

a. _____

b. _____

10. giving a minority report at a board of directors meeting

a. _____

b. _____

The Lord's hand was with them, and a great number of people believed and turned to the Lord.
Acts 11:21

SESSION 24

Speaking to the World (Part 1)

WARM-UP

When Jesus gave His apostles the master plan for spreading the Gospel to the world **(Acts 1:8),** they had a much different idea of the world than we do. In fact, our Lord, who knows all things, had in His mind the total picture of the world and all its billions of people. Imagine how the apostles would have reacted if they had known how large a world they were being sent into!

In this session we will look at one location in St. Paul's world of witnessing. We will visit the city of Ephesus. This city represents a cross section of the world of his time.

Paul arrived in Ephesus for the first time at the end of his second missionary journey. He found a strange mixture of Eastern and Western cultures. The West was represented by the Romans, who considered Ephesus an important commercial center. It was the western end of the major route through Asia Minor. Because of trade that used this route, the Romans, no doubt, realized great income.

It was therefore of concern to them that the harbor was beginning to silt up. Its loss would mean that trade might bypass Ephesus, and the city would decline in importance.

Eastern culture may have been more significant than Western culture in Ephesus, since the worship of an ancient Eastern goddess, Artemis (Diana), was centered here (see session 4). Trade increased because many pilgrims and tourists came to see the temple.

The worship of Artemis also brought brisk business in objects associated with magic, the occult, and prostitution. As trade through the harbor declined, revenue from the worship of Artemis increased.

Such was the world to which St. Paul addressed his letter to the Ephesians. Let us discover some of the events of Paul's ministry to this city.

FIRST HALF
Acts 19:1-22

After reading this section, complete the following sentences:

1. After some of the people frustrated Paul, he

_____

_____

2. The power of the Holy Spirit was seen in healings by means of

_____

_____

3. Through Paul and others, the power of Satan was broken. This was seen when

_____

_____

4. We find a summary of the growth and power of the Word in verse _____.

Verses 23-41

1. Demetrius and other craftsmen were upset with the Christians because

_____

_____

2. Paul's friends would not allow him to attend the hearing because

_____

_____

3. The city clerk (probably Roman) defended the Christians by saying that

_____

_____

4. He dismissed the meeting on grounds that

_____

_____

Ephesus and the World Today

In many ways this chapter summarizes how "called-out ones" find the world as they witness for the Lord Jesus Christ. Supply a geographic location today

THE GOSPEL TO THE WORLD

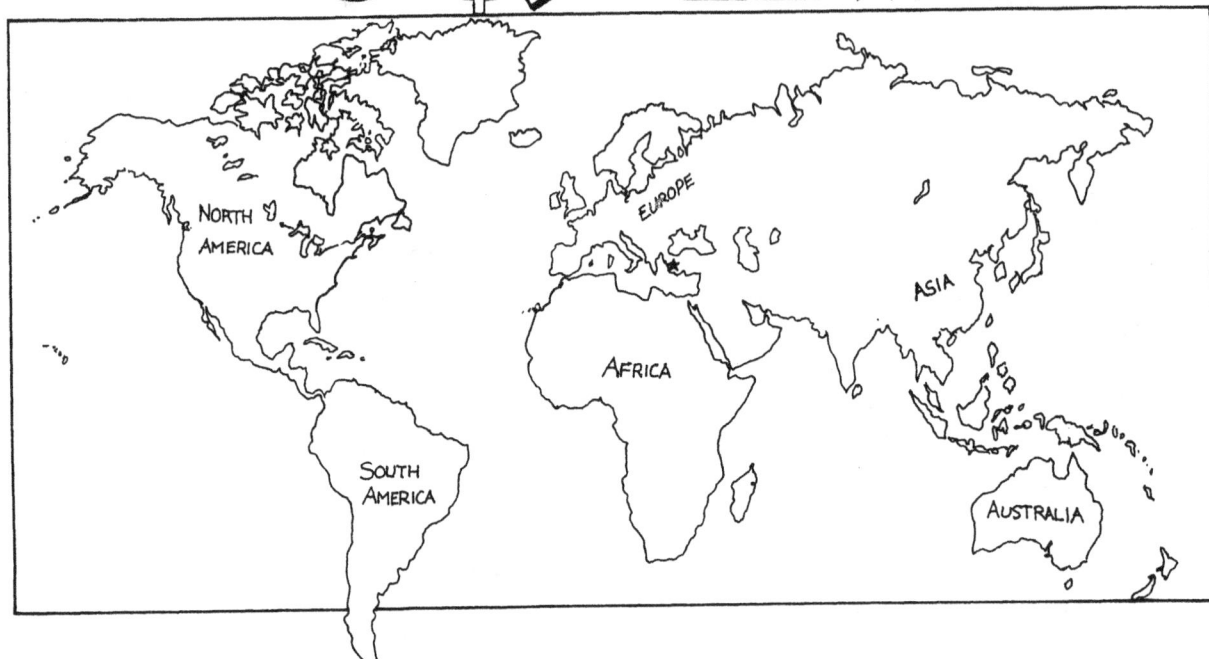

that is a parallel to the reaction found in Ephesus. Then explain why it is a good example.

1. A part of the world that has known the Gospel but rejects it because it does not fit its traditions **(verses 8-9)**.

2. A part of the world where the Gospel is accompanied by a medical ministry to people who desperately need physical care **(verses 11-12)**.

3. A part of the world where black magic and superstition are still practiced and where the Gospel has set many of these people free **(verses 17-19)**.

4. A part of the world where the Gospel is rejected and even outlawed because it does not further economic development and the distribution of wealth **(verses 23-26)**.

5. A part of the world where the Gospel is seen as opposing the local god; where believing in Christ, the Lord and Savior, would remove the worship of whatever else is in first place.

SECOND HALF

It's almost impossible for us individually to travel around the world to spread the Gospel. A local con-gregation is in a better position to do that. Usually, however, one congregation alone cannot do much because of the cost involved in supporting missionaries. So many congregations join together and form larger groups called *synods* or *associations.* With all the congregations contributing, a synod or association can then support such work.

1. Choose some of your class members to report on what is being done in the countries mentioned in the previous section. Contact your pastor or director of Christian education for information.

2. Our Lord Jesus told His disciples that the end of time would come only after the Gospel had been preached around the world **(Matt. 24:14)**. Using a wall map similar to the one reproduced here, trace the route that the Gospel has taken since St. Paul's day. Decide if, at this date, the Gospel has come full circle.

This gospel of the kingdom will be preached in the whole world as a testimony to all nations, and then the end will come.

Matthew 24:14

SESSION 25

Speaking to the World (Part 2)

WARM-UP

On the map in session 24 you drew arrows to show the progress of the Gospel through the world. Those arrows represent people—real people whose names are now forgotten, but not by the Lord. He remembers them with joy: those who brought the Gospel to the world. In this session we want to get acquainted with these real people: Christ's witnesses to the world.

FIRST HALF

You probably know of no greater witness for Christ than St. Paul. God's Word paints quite a picture of this special messenger of the Lord.

Let's piece together some of Paul's experiences.

1. Place of birth **(Acts 22:3)** _____

2. Studied under **(Acts 22:3)** _____

3. Place of conversion **(Acts 22:6-16)** _____

4. Baptized by **(Acts 22:6-16)** _____

5. Change of names **(Acts 13:9)** _____

6. List of hardships **(2 Corinthians 11:21b-28)**

   a. Number of beatings from Jews _____

   b. Number of beatings with rods _____

   c. Number of stonings _____

   d. Number of shipwrecks _____

   e. Time spent in sea _____

   f. Other hardships _____

   _____

   _____

7. Place of his first escape as a Christian **(2 Corinthians 11:30-33)** _____

8. Paul's name for an unknown illness **(2 Corinthians 12:7-10)** _____

9. God's answer to his prayer for healing **(2 Corinthians 12:7-10)** _____

10. Some of Paul's cherished possessions (2 Timothy 4:13) _____

11. Paul's philosophy (in your own words) (Philippians 3:7-9)

_____

_____

_____

_____

_____

SECOND HALF

What Paul did and had to say about himself has been duplicated countless times in the lives and philosophies of Christian missionaries. Today thousands of Christian missionaries labor around the world, just as Paul did.

Get a list of missionaries who are working overseas. Also try to find biographical material about them and a description of the type of ministry they conduct. Choose one and write a short letter to him or her.

These missionaries, of course, are busy people and have a limited amount of time for correspondence. But they love to receive mail. A letter from a fellow "called-out one" can do much to encourage them. Here are some suggestions for content:

1. Explain who you are and why you are writing. Be truthful.

2. Ask two or three questions about their work (joys, sorrows, etc.).

3. Add some personal word of encouragement of a spiritual nature. (Remember how Paul does it.)

4. Remember this person in your prayers. Tell them so.

5. Include your return home address. It might take some time, but you can expect an answer.

I consider [all things] rubbish, that I may gain Christ and be found in Him, not having a righteousness of my own that comes from the law, but that which is through faith in Christ—the righteousness that comes from God and is by faith.

Philippians 3:8b-9

SESSION 26

Witnessing by Imitation

WARM-UP

Imitate means to follow as a pattern, model, or example. Just think how often we imitate! A one-year-old toddler imitates sounds he hears from his parents. The three-year-old dresses up in her mother's old shoes and jewelry. The elementary-school student imitates favorite TV characters or sports heroes. We learn many of our basic skills by imitation!

List examples of imitation you find in music, food, fashion, sports, automobiles, and church.

Did the last category throw you? Whom or what do we imitate in church? In **Ephesians 5:1** St. Paul tells us to imitate God, to imitate the love He has for His children. In love God gave Himself into death for us. That is real love. That is how we are to imitate God.

What does imitating God have to do with witnessing? It's the means through which God gives added power to our words. Through this imitation others will **"praise your Father in heaven" (Matthew 5:16)**. When this happens, we become a letter from Christ, **"known and read by everybody" (2 Corinthians 3:2)**.

With that idea as a beginning, let us continue our study of how to be witnesses for Christ by imitation.

FIRST HALF

When we imitate God, others see God's love in our lives. St. Paul refers to some of these imitations when he writes to the Ephesians about ways "called-out ones" show God at work.

Imitation One: Unity (Ephesians 4:1-6)

1. Besides imitating the humbleness, gentleness, patience, and loving concern shown by Jesus, Paul stresses another quality of God, *oneness.* This quality is also stressed in **Deuteronomy 6:4: "Hear, O Israel: The Lord our God, the Lord is one."**

After Paul mentions this unity **(Ephesians 4:3)**, he proceeds to tell about the oneness God has given us. Fill in these blanks to tell more about this oneness.

One body is _____

One Spirit is _____

One hope of _____

One Lord is _____

One faith is _____

One baptism, consisting of _____

One God, called _____

2. Together, decide on four activities the church does that demonstrate its unity:

a. _____

b. _____

c. _____

d. _____

In sessions 30–31 we will look again at unity, the first of these imitations.

Imitation Two: Work (Verses 7-12a)

When Christ ascended to heaven, He removed His physical body from our view. In its place He put His church, the body of Christ. He accomplished His work through apostles, prophets, evangelists, pastors, and teachers.

1. For what purpose did God send these people to the church **(verse 12a)**?

_____

2. How can the church today imitate this work?

_____

_____

_____

_____

Imitation Three: Maturity
(Verses 12b-16)

Paul states the purpose of being unified in **verse 12b.**

1. Write this purpose in your own words.

_____

_____

Notice the emphasis on "called-out ones" becoming mature, gradually growing up to resemble Christ **(verse 13).**

2. Paul also refers to being a spiritual infant **(verse 14)** in **1 Corinthians 3:1-4.** How were these people acting like infants?

_____

_____

3. **"Speaking the truth in love" (verse 15)** is sometimes hard and requires maturity. Look up the following references. How does each demonstrate speaking the truth?

1 Samuel 20:24-33 _____

_____

Mark 8:31-33 _____

_____

Acts 15:1-2 _____

_____

Acts 21:10-14 _____

_____

4. Show how **Ephesians 4:16** summarizes the three imitations of God.

Unity _____

Work _____

Maturity _____

SECOND HALF

Our imitation of God presents a strong witness to the world. At times a silent example of the church's unity, of its members' work, and of the individual examples of Christian maturity seem to be more effective than many sermons.

In this activity you are to write a story, either true or fictional, to illustrate one of the three imitations of God. Make your story true to life. If you tell an actual incident, use fictitious names. Focus on what was done rather than on who did it.

Include in your story the effect that such a silent witness has on the world. Keep in mind Jesus' words in **Matthew 5:16: "that they may see your good deeds and praise your Father in heaven."**

Make your story long enough to be interesting and complete. Plan your beginning and ending carefully.

Following are some ideas to get you thinking creatively:

a. **On Unity:** The Best Game Our Team Ever Played; Local Church Destroyed by Fire; What Makes Lutheran High Schools Special? Local Students March for Hungry.

b. **On Jesus' Work:** John Jones, Team Manager; Carol's Visit to a Convalescent Hospital; Tom's Ministry at McDonald's; Found: One Wallet!

c. **On Christian Maturity:** No One Remembers Who Came in Second; "Sir, I Don't Agree!" A Clique that Cracked; A Language Lesson at Louie's.

Be imitators of God, therefore, as dearly loved children and live a life of love, just as Christ loved us and gave Himself up for us.

Ephesians 5:1-2

SESSION 27

Imitating at Home

WARM-UP

As we have examined St. Paul's teachings about the church, we have purposely avoided the most basic form of the church: the family. In the family, Christ's great command can be done in the most simple manner. **"Making disciples of all nations"** happens when both father and mother make little disciples of their children. **Baptizing them** is also the responsibility of the parents. So, as parents disciple and baptize, they are fulfilling Christ's command.

But the witness of a family church begins even before children appear. Both husband and wife have a witness to bring to each other—a witness by imitation. St. Paul continues this concept in **Ephesians 5—6** as he addresses husbands, wives, and children. Notice how he makes comparisons of model and imitator.

In an age when roles of husband and wife are being exchanged, and where both strive with each other for *equality,* a look at Paul's teaching is most enlightening. Skim **Ephesians 5:22-33** to get the drift of Paul's reasoning.

FIRST HALF
The Analogy

By now you know that Paul often uses comparisons to make his point. The great analogy or comparison of husband and wife is that Christ is like a husband and the church is like His bride. This is the basis for the lesson: husbands are to imitate Christ and wives are to imitate the church.

You will notice immediately that this analogy does away with equality. In no way is the church equal to Christ nor is Christ equal to the church. Both are unique, fulfilling a role ordained by God from eternity.

Christ is the Savior; He rescues His *damsel in distress.* He rushes in, snatches her away from the tyrant, Satan. But in doing so, He gives up His life for hers. As she pines for Him, He suddenly reappears, risen from the dead. He has defeated the false suitor, Satan. She is His forever. She now dedicates her life to Him, as He has given His life for her.

Since this relationship is based on unending love, there is absolutely no rivalry as to who is in charge. Christ has done and will do everything necessary to safeguard His bride and provide for her everything she needs. The church, owing her life to Christ, seeks ways to please and serve her Husband. When two people are completely in love with each other, rivalry disappears.

When outsiders peek into the window of Christ and His bride, they think they see domination and subservience. But the actions toward each other are really done as a result of love. When one has to dominate to get his or her way, that is not love, but selfishness. Christ and His bride are selfless, each living for the other.

Wives (Ephesians 5:22-24)

Now, when Paul uses the word **submit,** we understand. Submitting **as to the Lord** is just a way of receiving what in love the husband has to give to his wife. Christ gives only good gifts and makes only requests that are for the benefit of the church. Just so, a wife who imitates the church, will see only evidences of love in whatever her husband does for her and asks of her. What a noble, lofty position: to be the object of an undying love. This position can only be filled by a wife ready to see in her husband an imitation of Christ.

Husbands (Ephesians 5:25-33)

First, Paul says that husbands should love their wives to the point of giving up their own lives, if necessary. Then he makes another point. In **verse 28** he says, **"In this same way, husbands ought to love their wives as their own bodies. He who loves his wife loves himself."** Athletes train, lift weights, run, and diet to increase the value and use of the body. Just so, a husband will put himself through equal hardships in order for his wife to be happy.

Christ did it. He left home. He submitted to 33 years of humanity. He endured torture, ridicule, and the most shameful death. For what reason? To save His bride, the church.

Christian husbands will, as Paul says, feed and care for their bodies just as Christ feeds and cares for the church. Therefore, they will also do the same for their wives. This picture shows no attempt to dominate, just to give and care.

This is the kind of imitation God asks of a "called-out" husband or wife. It is a relationship based on giving and receiving, not on domination and submission.

But back to reality! How many husbands are truly Christlike? How many wives are like the church? No contest here. All husbands, all wives, fall short of the model. That is why Christ died. He forgives our sins. And we need to rely on **His** power even to approach that model. Then we *can* practice our imitations of the real thing, Christ and the church. In heaven we will finally get it right.

Children and Parents (Ephesians 6:1-4)

When Mom and Dad imitate Christ and the church, the love of Christ and the church affects the way they raise the children. They imitate the way God trains *His* children. Thus, God is actually training the children through God-fearing parents.

And now a word of caution. Being God's stand-ins might sound like a lofty position. It is. But it does not give parents the right to *exasperate* their children. Parents are not to make demands that God doesn't. They are not to change the ground rules to satisfy themselves, since God doesn't. They are not to frustrate their children eternally by neglecting instruction in God's Word. When parents imitate God the Father, they have a perfect model, and children will be cared for and taught as God would do it.

SECOND HALF

Perhaps you can now see how the family is a miniature church, with or without children. Your teacher will now ask questions on the reading in **Ephesians** and the explanation offered in this text. Your answers should be your own ideas. The goal for your answers should not be to score points, but to reflect on what God through Paul says about witnessing—witnessing through our imitations of Christ and the church.

[Gen. 2:24:]"For this reason a man will leave his father and mother and be united to his wife, and the two will become one flesh." This is a profound mystery—but I am talking about Christ and the church.

Ephesians 5:31-32

SESSION 28

Before and After

WARM-UP

Most of us enjoy the *Before and After* features in magazines. You've probably seen, for example, a black-and-white picture of a dowdy, sullen looking, frumpy individual. Next to it, you see a living-color photo of a smiling, vibrant creature looking at least 20 years younger.

Or maybe you remember that snapshot of the old beat-up heap out behind the garage. Dings and dents cover every part of the rusted body. Internal problems must exist, because the springs sag and the hood doesn't fit. But sure enough, after long hours of labor and tons of money, there stands the shiny, fully restored, classic antique. Yes, before-and-after is fun, especially when the after is a vast improvement over the before!

In our next step in imitating God, St. Paul presents us with a before-and-after situation. This one does not involve a hair style or a paint job. This is an internal restoration, done by the Lord Himself. The objects are the members of the Ephesians' congregation. Our text is **Ephesians 4:17-32.**

FIRST HALF
Ephesians 4:17-19

This is a description of the life-style of those whom Paul calls Gentiles. Today we would call them unbelievers: those who either have not heard the Gospel or those who, having heard it, have rejected it.

1. A *buzzword* is a word that carries strong meaning and excites the emotions. Paul uses such buzzwords in describing the activities of the unbelievers. Write the words and phrases that describe the unbelieving life-style.

_____

2. These phrases describe the "before" condition of the Ephesians. Since many of us cannot remember not living in the faith, we can only wonder what that kind of life can be like. Following are two incidents that illustrate what that life-style is like: **Judges 1; 2 Kings**

21:1-9. After reading them, help the class list the buzzwords from 1 that you observed.

Verses 20-24

1. The changeover comes with conversion through the power of the Holy Spirit. Whether it began at your baptism as a child or in later life, we all belonged in that old life-style. Paul compares the changeover to putting off your old self and putting on a fresh new self. Write the description of this new self.

_____

_____

This new self is similar to a new set of clothes. Read the parable of the wedding banquet in **Matthew 22:1-14.**

2. How is the garment provided by the king like the new self created by God?

_____

3. Why was the king justified in throwing out the man who wouldn't wear it?

_____

Verses 25-32

You might recognize Paul's list of changes as restatements of some of the Ten Commandments. For a new self, created by God, this list is proof that new life exists. In addition, Paul gives another reason for doing each commandment. After each item, write
    a. The number of the commandment.
    b. The other reason for doing it.
    1. Speaking truthfully

a._____

b. _____

    2. Being angry

a._____

b. _____

    3. Doing useful work

a. _____

b. _____

    4. Helpful talk

a. _____

b. _____

    5. Forgiving

a. _____

b. _____

SECOND HALF

1. All the actions Paul mentions in **verses 25-32,** both positive and negative, occur also in local congregations. We want to concentrate on the positive ones, since they bear a strong witness to fellow believers.

Among "called-out ones" these actions occur every day. They often happen without "called-out ones" realizing it. In this activity, you are to recall such incidents. They take place in the adult world as well as in the teenage world. After each item:

a. List something a teenager has done. (If necessary, ask your teacher to supply this.)

b. List something an adult has done.

Speaking truthfully

a. _____

b. _____

Being angry

a. _____

b. _____

Doing useful work for others

a. _____

b. _____

Helpful talk

a. _____

b. _____

Forgiving

a. _____

b. _____

2. While we are in a storytelling mood, take turns reading the story you wrote in session 26. You will notice that these stories are on the same subject—witnessing by imitation. As you listen, try to pick out some of the five positive signs we have just been discussing.

You were taught, with regard to your former way of life, to put off your old self, which is being corrupted by its deceitful desires; to be made new in the attitude of your minds; and to put on the new self, created to be like God in true righteousness and holiness.

Ephesians 4:22-23

SESSION 29

Imitating the Light

WARM-UP

St. Paul did not have an easy job. Of course, we know that already. But his most difficult job was not preaching. It was being an imitator of God. Perhaps he was thinking about some of those difficult times when he wrote in **Ephesians 5:1-2: "Be imitators of God, therefore, as dearly loved children and live a life of love, just as Christ loved us and gave Himself up for us as a fragrant offering and sacrifice to God."**

One of the difficult imitations of God occurred in Philippi as recorded in **Acts 16:16-40.** Read that story now and make a list of the imitations of God that Paul and Silas did. After reading, share with your class those you found.

We have read some of what Paul says about imitating God. He says more about it in **Ephesians 5:3-21.**

FIRST HALF
Ephesians 5:8-14

Let's begin in the middle of our reading for a change. Paul's frame of reference here is *light* and *darkness.* He calls the "before" Ephesians *dark* and the "after" Ephesians *light.* People have always equated darkness with evil. Even with today's marvels of artificial light, we still relate evil to darkness and good to light.

1. To illustrate this, match the words from the text with the contemporary parallels listed here. Be ready to point out the similarity.
   a. Parking
   b. Photosynthesis
   c. Songbirds at dawn
   d. Streetlights
   e. Mushrooms

_____Live as children of light (verse 8)

_____The fruit of the light consists in all goodness (verse 9)

_____Fruitless deeds of darkness (verse 11)

_____What the disobedient do in secret (verse 12)

_____Everything exposed by the light becomes visible (verse 13)

2. Read **John 1:6-9.** How did the "after" Ephesians become light?

_____

3. What message from **Isaiah 60:1-3** does Paul quote?

_____

Verses 3-7

Read these verses. Then discuss the following questions.

1. In **verse 5,** Paul states that **"no immoral, impure or greedy person . . . has any inheritance in the kingdom of Christ."** Does this mean that anyone who has sinned against the 6th Commandment will not be saved? Give reasons for your position.

2. What examples in Scripture illustrate **verses 6-7?**

3. Paul speaks about immorality in **verses 3-4.** Use the examples Paul names. Have the best mimic in the class mime a person passing along an obscene story or looking at a dirty book. Notice how the actions show the need for secrecy or darkness.

4. This should help to answer 1 in this section. At times people of the light do sin in the ways described by Paul. How, then, can we call them people of the light? It's because of what happens afterwards. People of the light, when they realize what they have done, immediately seek out the light—the forgiveness in Christ. People of the dark, on the other hand, scuttle further into the dark, trying to hide even farther away from the Lord. Pick out phrases in **verses 8-14** that describe the direction people of the light take after sin.

Verses 15-21

This section says more about light. Of course, the organs of light are the eyes. One translation of **verse 15 (RSV)** says, **"Look carefully then how you walk."**

For each organization and each style, see if Paul's two purposes are of primary importance.

Organizations	Styles
_____	_____
_____	_____
_____	_____
_____	_____
_____	_____
_____	_____

5. When people in the church disagree about how music should be done in the church and which music should be used, how can the matter be settled? What advice does **verse 21** provide?

SECOND HALF

Discuss the various kinds of music with which the church has been blessed.

Whether you like or dislike various styles of Christian music, you will have to agree that the Lord has provided great variety for us today. We have the opportunity to sing a hymn that has existed for over 1,600 years and a Christian rock song just released!

We imitate the light when we sing and make music in our hearts to the Lord. Such music can only be written and performed in the light of Christ.

Wake up, O sleeper, rise from the dead, and Christ will shine on you.

Ephesians 5:14

In other words, Paul tells the Ephesians to live in the light, with eyes of faith wide open, all senses on the alert.

Discuss the following questions:

1. How can doing the following send a person of the light into the dark?

a. being foolish **(verse 17)**

b. getting drunk **(verse 18)**

2. In **verses 19-20** Paul speaks of Christian music. What motivation does he give for sacred music?

3. He expressed the same idea in **Colossians 3:15-16.** What added purpose for Christian music did Paul give there?

4. List various musical organizations in the church. Also list the many styles of Christian music available.

SESSION 30
The Ultimate Imitation

WARM-UP

Someone has said, "Imitation is the sincerest form of flattery." One does not need to look far to see that this is true.

A TV show captures the top ratings during a season; the following season several similar shows appear. A pro team has a winning season; suddenly everyone wears its T-shirts and buys its souvenirs. A music group makes it big; soon we find look-alike and sound-alike groups.

In the church we also find one ultimate imitation. Without even trying, God's "called-out ones" demonstrate the greatest imitation of God's love. Read **Ephesians 3:1-6** to find out what it is.

FIRST HALF
Ephesians 3:1-6

First read just **verse 1.** As Paul finishes this verse, he stops in midsentence, suddenly taken with a wondrous thought. The combination of his being a captive to the life of Christ with his being a witness to the Gentiles triggers a great idea. Paul calls this idea *grace.* We learned that grace is God's undeserved kindness to sinful humanity. That is what Paul wants to think about—God's grace, but on a bigger scale.

Now read **verses 2-6.** In this section we find the ultimate imitation. Paul begins by remembering God's grace to him personally.

1. How was God's grace given to Paul?

_____

_____

2. What do the following readings all have in common? **Acts 9:1-5; 16:6-10; 27:21-25; Galatians 1:11-12** and **2 Corinthians 12:7-9.**

_____

_____

3. Apparently God also did this for the other apostles. What great mystery did He now reveal?

_____

_____

4. This may not seem like much of a mystery to us, because we have always known it. But this was a major change to the first-century Christians. Look up the following references and notice how the pieces were fitted into the mystery as God unfolded His plan of salvation. Write the phrase that develops a part of the mystery.

a. **Genesis 12:2-3:** _____

_____

b. **Isaiah 60:1-3:** _____

_____

c. **Matthew 8:5-12:** _____

_____

d. **John 10:14-16:** _____

_____

e. **Luke 24:45-48:** _____

_____

f. **Acts 11:11-18:** _____

_____

5. Read the description of this mystery in **Ephesians 4:4-6.** According to this, what is the church's ultimate imitation of God?

_____

_____

John 17

Jesus spoke many times of this mystery. We find a deep and beautiful expression of this mystery is the *High-Priestly Prayer* (**John 17**). Read this prayer and answer the questions below.

1. How did Jesus express His unity with the Father?

_____

_____

2. How did Jesus express His unity with the disciples?

_____

_____

3. How did Jesus express the unity of Father with Son, with the apostles, and with future "called-out ones"?

_____

_____

4. Finally, what does Jesus request to be the ultimate state of "His called out-ones"?

_____

_____

SECOND HALF

1. Today we express this ultimate imitation of God in many ways. We refer to the church as *The Holy Christian Church; the Communion of Saints; the Holy Catholic Church; the Invisible Church; the Kingdom of Grace; the Church Militant.* All of these terms refer to the church, but each has a slightly different emphasis. Ask your teacher to help you find the particular meaning of each term:

The Holy Christian Church
The Communion of Saints
The Holy Catholic Church
The Invisible Church
The Kingdom of Grace
The Church Militant

2. Many Christian hymns have been written about the church. Find some in your hymnal that refer to the unity of the church. You might begin with the second stanza of "The Church's One Foundation."

Hymn Title	Unity Quote
The Church's One Foundation	from every nation, yet one; one Lord, one faith, one birth; one name; one food; one hope.
_____	_____
	_____
_____	_____
	_____
_____	_____
_____	_____
	_____
_____	_____
	_____
_____	_____
_____	_____
	_____
_____	_____
	_____
_____	

This grace was given to me: to preach to the Gentiles the unsearchable riches of Christ, and to make plain to everyone the administration of this mystery.

Ephesians 3:8-9

SESSION 31

Many Imitations

WARM-UP

Did you feel in the last session that there was more to the story? There is. Unfortunately, we find some negative aspects to the rest of the story. We find that, in spite of Jesus' prayer for unity, the church is outwardly divided. God's church still consists of "called-out ones" who trust in Christ for salvation, but many of these "called-out ones" choose to be separated from others in the practice of their faith.

You will probably have an opportunity to learn more about how this came to be during another course. This simple picture, however, may help you get an overview of what the church looks like outwardly.

This diagram, of course, oversimplifies a very complex history. It does not show which branch is the strongest, the largest, or the straightest. We can, however, draw some conclusions based on this diagram:

1. All branches are still connected to the root, which is Christ. Therefore we can expect to find "called-out ones" in each branch.

2. The various branches show the work of sin. Without sin we would find a unified church.

During this session you will learn something of how these divisions took place. You will also see how, in spite of the divisions, the Holy Spirit still accomplishes His work.

FIRST HALF

One of the symptoms of sin is its power to divide. Consider these examples:

—After sinning, Adam and Eve chose to hide from God **(Genesis 3:8).**

—Sin divided Abel from Cain, and after his sin Cain was divided from the rest of the first family **(Genesis 4:1-16).**

—The sin of pride caused God to confuse the languages of humanity at Babel **(Genesis 11:1-9).**

1. Even in the early church, the seeds of division were present. All were the result of sin. Look up the following references and write what the division was about and who was involved.

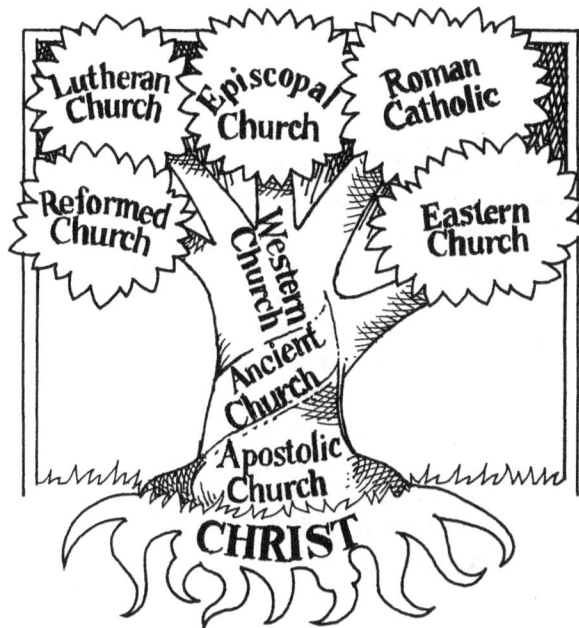

a. **Acts 6:1** _____

_____

b. **Galatians 2:11-14** _____

_____

c. **Acts 15:36-41** _____

_____

d. **1 Corinthians 1:10-17** _____

_____

2. These divisions, of course, occurred because of sin. Paul gets to the heart of the problem in the following references. After you read a reference, write a brief answer to the accompanying question.

a. **Ephesians 3:7-11:** What is God's main task for the church? _____

_____

b. **Colossians 2:16-19:** This text obviously speaks of examples of false teachings and divisive beliefs. What analogy does Paul use in **verse 19** to explain these false teachings?

c. **Romans 16:17-19:** Who, in this text, is disconnected from the Head? How can one know who is disconnected?

_____

_____

d. **1 John 4:1-3:** What test does John suggest to determine if a teaching is true or false?

_____

_____

3. After reading about the causes of divisions, you still do not have an answer to the question, "Which division (denomination) is the best one?" You will not find anything in Scripture that says, "The Lutheran (Roman Catholic, Baptist, etc.) Church is the best." But you will find many passages that indicate how you can test a denomination to see how well it measures up.

One such passage is **Ephesians 3:7-13.** Read this thoughtfully and carefully. Think of it as a measuring device for denominations. Then answer these questions for your own denomination.

a. **Verses 7-8a:** What does it teach of humanity's sin and God's grace?

_____

_____

b. **Verses 8b-9:** What is its main purpose for existence?

_____

_____

c. **Verse 10:** On what does it base its message?

_____

_____

d. **Verse 11:** How important is the person and work of Jesus Christ?

_____

_____

e. **Verse 12:** How important is faith in our relationship with God?

_____

_____

f. **Verse 13:** How does it view the suffering of its own members?

_____

_____

Obviously, the branch (denomination) that best meets these needs is the one to which you should belong. To help you see this better, work through **"Second Half."**

SECOND HALF

With your teacher and class, list those denominations that are of interest to you. For each, determine answers to the following categories based on **Ephesians 3:7-13.**

    A. Sin and Grace *   D. Importance of Christ *
    B. Purpose **   E. Importance of Faith *
    C. Message Source *   F. Purpose of Suffering **

  *Key doctrines God has given to His church
  ** Responses we make to God

Make use of your experience as well as the input of your teacher.

If needed, plan to use more time on this activity as questions arise about other denominations.

I urge you, brothers, to watch out for those who cause divisions and put obstacles in your way that are contrary to the teaching you have learned. Keep away from them.

                                              Romans 16:17

SESSION 32

Witnessing by Giving

WARM-UP

The mail had just come. Mrs. Anderson quickly thumbed through the envelopes to see what she should open first. There were the usual ads—a free car wash and a grand opening of a new pizza parlor—and the usual Tuesday envelope of manufacturer's coupons.

Then came the bills, right on time: the gas bill, the phone bill, and the big one—car insurance.

Finally, she sorted out the items she had questions about: a blue window-envelope with no return address except for the title, "Office of the Auditor." Next was a hand-addressed business size envelope with the return address of her congregation. Last was a business envelope addressed "To the Parents of Jenny Anderson." The return address: Jenny's high school!

Can you guess what was in each of the last three letters? Compare your guesses with those of the rest of your class. According to your guesses, which one of the three would Mrs. Anderson open last? Why?

Did you guess the letter from her congregation? In fact, she opened it after the bills and just before the ads. Mrs. Anderson correctly guessed that the congregation letter was an appeal for increased giving. As she stuffed it into the desk drawer, she muttered, "They're always asking for money. The only time you hear from the church is when they want something."

Maybe Mrs. Anderson is right. But shouldn't the church ask us to give something? Think about that question as you read what Paul has to say to the Corinthian Christians in **2 Corinthians 8:1-15.**

FIRST HALF

True-False Statements

After reading **2 Corinthians 8:1-15,** tell whether the following statements are true or false.

1. ____ The Macedonian congregations were suffering some trial but at the same time were giving generously for the needs of the saints.

2. ____ These congregations gave because Paul had pleaded with them to be generous.

3. ____ The first gift given to the Lord by the Macedonian congregation was their heart.

4. ____ The act of giving, according to Paul, is solely a result of God's grace.

5. ____ Paul had instructed Titus to tell the Corinthians how generous the Macedonians had been so that the Corinthians might be moved to give also.

6. ____ Paul equates giving with other acts of faith such as love, faith, knowledge, speech, and earnestness.

7. ____ Christ is an example of giving because as God's Son He was rich and gave out His richness to us who are comparatively poor.

8. ____ The Corinthian congregation apparently needed this reminder to give, because other congregations had given first and Paul did not want them to be the last to begin.

9. ____ Paul expected the Corinthians to give up their possessions so that other congregations would not have to.

10. ____ Just as God supplied the needs of the Israelites in the wilderness, God supplies the needs of His people today through the gifts of other "called-out ones."

11. ____ Since God does not mention tithing in the New Testament, we should not encourage one another to tithe.

Discuss the answers to this quiz with your classmates. Don't just talk, though, about whether a statement is true or false. Rather, discuss the reasons for your answers.

Unfinished Sentences

On the basis of your discussion, complete the following sentences.

1. God expects all of His children, rich or poor, to give of their possessions because

_____

2. God is not pleased with people's gifts unless

_____

_____

3. The one and only motivation for true giving is

_____

4. God does not need our gifts, but we need to give them to God because

_____

_____

5. If a "called-out one" does not give to the Lord, it means that

_____

_____

SECOND HALF

Fund-raising today is a big business. Congregations, parochial high schools, colleges, and charitable organizations seemingly could not exist without an organized program of gift encouragement. In an effort to raise as much as possible, highly organized methods have been developed. Some of them run dangerously close to asking for gifts for the wrong reasons.

Below are some common fund-raising methods. After reading each description, decide (on the basis of today's Bible study) if gifts raised in this way are pleasing to God.

1. *The Sealed Pledge:* The giver is asked to estimate the amount of his or her gift for the coming year. The pledge is sealed and opened only by the giver at the end of the year.

2. *The Contribution Report:* No special fund-raising drive is conducted. At the end of the giving period a report is published containing names of all members and what they gave.

3. *The Walk-a-Thon:* Students and others from a charitable organization ask friends to sponsor them. To do this, the would-be giver is asked to pledge a certain amount for each lap or mile walked.

4. *The Bake Sale:* Students or others make baked goods and sell them. All proceeds are given to the organization.

5. *The Raffle:* Students or others sell chances on some large item like a car or VCR. The person with the number drawn gets the prize. All proceeds go to the organization.

6. *The Auction:* Businesses and individuals donate items and services to be auctioned off to friends and supporters of an organization. Proceeds go to the organization. Businesses and individuals may deduct the value of their donation from income tax.

7. *The Phon-a-Thon:* Volunteers make numerous personal calls to people on a prepared list of names. All funds received go to the organization.

Excel in this grace of giving. . . . For you know the grace of our Lord Jesus Christ, that though He was rich, yet for your sakes He became poor, so that you through His poverty might become rich.
2 Corinthians 8:7b, 9

SESSION 33

Witnessing by Receiving

WARM-UP

What do you do and how do you feel when you receive a compliment? To help you find out, your teacher will begin an activity during which members of your class receive compliments. These should not be fake. If you choose to give a compliment, be sure it's genuine—that it's a compliment someone in your class deserves. Perhaps you will get one also.

What happened when you and your classmates were complimented? Did you feel embarrassed? Did your classmates? If so, why did you? What is it that causes us to say such things as "It was really nothing" or "Anyone could have done it"?

When we receive an unexpected gift we sometimes say, "Oh, you shouldn't have done it." When accepting a dinner invitation, many people feel obligated to give the host and hostess a gift. When we get a Christmas card from someone but didn't send one to that person, many of us either quickly send one or feel guilty.

What about the church? We have received and continue to receive so many good things from our heavenly Father. How do we receive them? As described above, or is there a difference?

St. Paul was on the receiving end of a gift from the congregation at Philippi. Paul may have been referring to these people and their gifts to him in **2 Corinthians 8** (the reading for session 32). Read Paul's reaction to this gift in **Philippians 4:10-20.**

FIRST HALF

Philippians 4:13

Again we will begin in the middle of the reading. Again Paul highlights the Source of all good things: **through Him** (God). List five things you remember from your study of Paul's life and writings that the *Lord gave him* power to do.

1. _____

2. _____

3. _____

4. _____

5. _____

Verses 10-12 and 14-20

Paul acknowledges the care and concern shown him by the Philippian Christians. But instead of saying, "You shouldn't have done it," he says that he rejoices in the Lord because they did help him. He recognized that their gift was God's way of caring for him. This leads to the second characteristic of one who receives from God: *contentment.*

1. Read the following references. Be ready to summarize the needs Paul had and to tell how God helped him.

   a. **Acts 9:7-19**

   b. **Acts 14:19-20**

   c. **Acts 16:14-15**

   d. **Galatians 4:12-14**

   e. **Acts 27:39-44**

2. Now read these references. They indicate that occasionally Paul was rather well off. Be ready to tell where Paul was and how he was well cared for.

   a. **Acts 22:3**

   b. **Acts 28:30-31**

   c. **Philippians 4:14-19**

3. Paul says he has learned the secret of being content. What is it?

_____

_____

Verses 4-7

Being a receiver of God's gifts not only enables one to recognize God as the Giver and therefore to be content. We can also be *completely happy and at peace.*

1. Write the words that show Paul's happiness with God.

_____

_____

2. Write the words that show the complete peace he felt.

_____

_____

_____

That's it! That's how to be a receiver of God's gifts:
Recognize where they came from
Be satisfied
Be happy

Notice that we find no feeling of guilt, no desire to settle up, no false humbleness. God encourages us to respond to His goodness with a big "Thank You" in word and deed.

SECOND HALF

1. In **Ephesians 5:20** Paul tells us to give thanks always to God the Father for everything. This is the "called-out one's" way of receiving God's blessings, even those that don't look like blessings. Even during a very bad situation, God provides reasons for us to thank Him.

Paul did. For instance, in **Philippians 1:12-14** Paul tells about good that came about because he became a prisoner in Rome. The palace guard heard the Gospel and other Christians became more bold to speak up for Christ.

In **2 Corinthians 12:7-10** Paul mentions his mysterious "thorn," some burden that God would not remove. So, in **verse 10,** Paul states that he now delights in weaknesses, insults, hardships, persecutions, and difficulties because **"when I am weak, then I am strong."** He is strong because He trusts God's sustaining help.

Can you find good in a tough situation? Talk about those that follow. Look for a blessing from God in each one. All names and situations are fictitious. The people in these incidents are "called-out ones."

a. Joe Brown, a promising athlete, has received many athletic scholarship offers. He is severely injured in a car accident and has lost the use of his legs.

b. Kathleen Donovan's father dies when she is only 7. She, her sister, and mother move in with the grandparents. Her grandfather is a pastor.

c. St. John's congregation is in a changing neighborhood. Many of the old members have died or moved away. The newcomers tend to be poor, largely uneducated, and not acquainted at all with St. John's church or school.

d. Lutheran High's basketball team makes it to the state finals. In a hard-fought game, they lose to a team from a small rural town.

2. So much for large troubles and even larger blessings. Make up a blessing that comes from each of the following.

a. an F
b. a flat tire
c. breaking up
d. being grounded
e. a cut in working hours
f. being turned down or not asked for a date
g. a divorce
h. unfair treatment
i. a youth group that does nothing
j. a prayer that God does not seem to answer

I am amply supplied, now that I have received from Epaphroditus the gifts you sent. They are a fragrant offering, an acceptable sacrifice, pleasing to God.
Philippians 4:18

SESSION 34

Where Do Our Gifts Go?

WARM-UP

In this unit we have concentrated on the church's witness by word and deed. In all of these details we could lose sight of the purpose of our witness.

Sometimes we are tempted to speak about Christ just to gain congregation members. Sometimes we are tempted to give money because if we don't, the local congregation or school might not have enough money. Sometimes we are tempted to imitate the love of God because that's what others expect of us.

While these reasons border on the truth, they miss the main point. As you have read during previous sessions, we act in love because Jesus acted in love for us. His love moves us to imitate Him in word and deed. Jesus told about these imitations in **Matthew 25:31-40.** He described an event as it will happen, an event in which all "called-out ones" will participate. Jesus speaks here of the first gathering of the entire church of all time.

FIRST HALF
Matthew 25:31-34

In this account Jesus describes the event we call *Judgment Day*. Actually, *Separation Day* might be a better title, since the context does not suggest a trial. All nations will be present—the same "all nations" that Jesus told His "called-out ones" to make disciples of.

With no questions asked and no defenses given, Christ the King will separate the nations, just as a shepherd at the end of the day would bar the doorway to the sheepfold. He will allow only the sheep in, but the goats who had infiltrated the flock will be kept out. There certainly won't be any question about which is a sheep and which is a goat, just as there will be no question about who is a "called-out one" and who isn't. That judgment has already occurred. At this point, Christ merely completes the separation.

1. Read Jesus' parable in **Matthew 13:24-30.** Write how this parable explains what Jesus does on *Separation Day.*

_____

2. How do we know from the context of both **Mat-**
thew 25:34 and **Matthew 13:24-30** that entrance into eternal life with Christ is by His grace alone?

_____

_____

3. What does each of these passages say about the way we are saved?

John 3:16	**Romans 3:23-24**
Romans 1:17	**Ephesians 2:8-10**

Verses 35-40

It is obvious, then, that those on Jesus' right are the "called-out ones," the church. Notice what Christ says to His chosen ones.

1. List the six curses of sin that Jesus mentions that have afflicted humanity since Adam and Eve sinned.

a. _____ d. _____

b. _____ e. _____

c. _____ f. _____

2. God's children then reply that they weren't aware of times when they had addressed these needs. Can you? Give one example for each of the six needs, where an individual, a congregation, or an association has supplied help.

a. _____

b. _____

c. _____

d. _____

e. _____

f. _____

3. Jesus answers: **"Whatever you did for one of the least of these brothers of Mine, you did for Me".**

When we go about our business of witnessing by word and deed, Jesus says, we are really doing all of it for and to Him. This fits exactly with what Paul has been telling us repeatedly. Look up the following ref-

erences. Rephrase what Paul says about what we do for Christ.

a. **Romans 12:1** _____

_____

b. **1 Corinthians 10:31** _____

_____

c. **2 Corinthians 8:5** _____

_____

d. **Galatians 4:14** _____

_____

e. **Ephesians 6:5** _____

_____

f. **Colossians 3:17** _____

_____

4. Write a short paragraph explaining why you, as a "called-out one," want to give help to those in need.

_____

_____

SECOND HALF

Imagine what it would be like to do each of the six things Jesus mentioned. Have you ever visited a prison? (Jesus didn't mean a prison visit for a field trip. He meant a visit to a convicted "bad person.") Performing these acts of love may not be fun of itself. The fun comes from the joy we get whenever we do anything for the Lord.

As a class activity, share your experiences or those that you have heard about concerning the following.

1. *What is it like to starve?* Over half the world's population does not receive enough to eat. What is being done to solve world hunger?

2. *What are the effects of drought?* Consider northern Africa or our own dust bowl of the 1930s. Consider also the dangers of water pollution. How can we help solve the shortage of usable water?

3. *Where are the homeless and how are they cared for?* What is it like to sleep out on the street? Who are the "strangers" among us that need taking in?

4. *What happens to the clothes we don't want anymore?* What opportunities do we have to give clothing to those who need it?

5. *What is the difference between "visiting" and "looking after" the sick?* Think of life in a convalescent home. How will you care for your parents when they can't care for themselves?

6. *What mission work can be done in the state penitentiary?* What is our attitude toward those convicted of crime? How can you help someone in other "penitentiaries," such as being isolated from friendships because of past behavior?

I tell you the truth, whatever you did for one of the least of these brothers of Mine, you did for Me.
Matthew 25:40

SESSION 35

Concluding Activities for Unit 5

Below are statements that summarize the main points of this unit's sessions. Please write a question that would lead to each answer. Write your questions on a separate sheet of paper.

1. Source of power: Holy Spirit; occupation: witnesses; order of progression: home, surrounding areas, world. (Session 21.)

2. Seventy elders of Israel, Samson, King Saul, Ezekiel, Zechariah, the apostles, the family of Cornelius, and 12 men from Ephesus are all examples. (Session 21.)

3. In **John 4,** Jesus demonstrates how to be a fisher of men by speaking to a woman of Samaria and proclaiming to her the Gospel. (Session 22.)

4. The three devices used by Jesus are the bait, the hook, and the line and pole. The bait is an interest-getter, the hook is the Law, the line and pole are the Gospel. (Session 22.)

5. It can do this by being led by a faithful pastor who will encourage the members to witness, to help, and to be Christ's presence in the neighborhood. (Session 23.)

6. Ephesus was dominated by materialism, the cult of Artemis, immorality, and sorcery. The same problems plague the world today. (Sessions 24 and 25.)

7. Because of the expense and difficulty of supporting world missions, congregations join together in voluntary associations to do Christ's work together. (Sessions 24 and 25.)

8. By being unified in work, hope, faith, maturity, and love, the church accomplishes this through the Spirit. (Session 26.)

9. When the husband imitates the love of Christ and the wife imitates the willingness of the church to serve, they demonstrate the analogy Paul presents in **Ephesians 5.** (Session 27.)

10. After conversion the righteousness of God covers a person's life. We do the things God would have us do. (Session 28.)

11. When people of the light sin, they seek to get closer to the light of God's forgiveness. People of the dark retreat farther and farther into the darkness of sin. (Session 29.)

12. In **John 17** Jesus prays that His followers may be one just as He is one with His Father and with His disciples. (Session 30.)

13. This reference expresses concern for the teaching of sin and grace, its purpose, the basis for its message, the importance of Christ and faith in Him, and the place of suffering in the lives of its members. (Session 31.)

14. This is acceptable only as a "thanks" for God's grace in Christ. It is a true expression of the heart of a "called-out one." (Session 32.)

15. When the church helps those in need, it is really giving to the Lord. He does not need our gifts, but sees them as fruit of a thankful heart. (Sessions 33 and 34.)

UNIT 6:

Conflict and Victory

Why don't athletes like to sit on the bench? They certainly won't get hurt. They won't get yelled at for making mistakes. They are a part of the team and enjoy the benefits of team membership. But they miss one benefit—they don't get to play!

It's exciting to be a part of a contest. Win or lose, there is no substitute for competition. And you can't experience that on the bench!

As members of the church we are part of a different kind of conflict. First of all, it's not a game. And we're all in this conflict; there is no bench. The conflict is with Satan. We know his purpose: to deceive the church. He wants believers to give up their life with Christ and live his way.

In this final unit you will learn about challenges in this contest. You will discover where and how Satan fights. You will learn what God has given you to fight against him. Best of all, you will experience the joy of victory as St. Paul and St. John describe it.

Have you ever been a member of a team where you **knew** you would win? Christ assures us that through Him we are the winners over Satan, death, and sin. In the final session you will discover the eternal reward that awaits you in heaven. Finally, you will celebrate this victory with your classmates in a special worship experience.

Since the last five sessions (41—45) stress the victory that is ours in Christ, the names of each part of the session will reflect this. We will begin with **"Final Whistle,"** where conflict stops and victory fun begins. This will be followed by **"Celebration."** We celebrate through learning and practicing. Think of it as practice in living with Christ forever.

St. Paul often looked forward to being with Christ forever. The church also looks forward to the day when it can throw down its battle manual and begin the eternal song of praise. And so rejoice with St. John in the words of **Revelation 22:20: "He who testifies to these things says, 'Yes, I am coming soon.' Amen. Come, Lord Jesus."**

SESSION 36

Recognizing the Enemy

WARM-UP

Athletics are exciting and worthwhile activities. But sooner or later we have to face the fact that the game is over. The outcome has been decided, and life continues. The ecstasy of victory and the agony of defeat fade away. The world will be little affected by the outcome of our games.

But that's not true of the topic of this session. We're talking about a life and death struggle, not a game. The stakes involve our eternal destiny. And there are no spectators. We are all involved, whether we know it or not, whether we want to be or not.

Our "contest" is life. The stakes involve where you will eternally live it. The opponents are the "called-out ones" (the church) versus the "kicked-out ones" (the devil and his evil spirits).

This session will fill you in on the background of this struggle. The Lord in His wisdom has seen fit not to reveal all the details of it, since our salvation depends on Christ and His victory, and not on our knowledge of all the eternal details. The Lord has sprinkled little bits and pieces of this struggle throughout Scripture. Therefore we will examine various references.

FIRST HALF

The Struggle Then

We will pretend that newspapers have covered this struggle. Below are headlines as they may have appeared in a celestial newspaper. Match the headlines with the references.

a. CHRIST, FOLLOWERS DEFEAT SATAN AND DEATH
b. CHRIST MAKES VICTORIOUS VISIT TO HELL
c. FIRST FAMILY TRICKED BY SERPENT
d. MESSIAH DIES IN CALVARY SHOWDOWN
e. MESSIAH, SATAN MEET IN SKIRMISH
f. SATAN GOES ON PROWL
g. SERPENT, WOMAN'S OFFSPRING TO MEET IN MORTAL COMBAT
h. WAR IN HEAVEN—SATAN EXPELLED

i. WOMAN'S OFFSPRING APPEARS AS PROMISED

_____ 1. **Revelation 12:7-9**

_____ 2. **1 Peter 5:8**

_____ 3. **Genesis 3:1-6**

_____ 4. **Genesis 3:12-15**

_____ 5. **Galatians 4:4-5**

_____ 6. **Matthew 4:1-11**

_____ 7. **Philippians 2:8**

_____ 8. **1 Peter 3:18-19**

_____ 9. **1 Corinthians 15:20-23**

The Struggle Now

Christ has won the victory over Satan and death. But how many people know it? How many "called-out ones" day by day are aware that Satan has lost? This is what Satan is counting on—that he can trick Christ's followers into coming over to the losing side.

And so the struggle continues. The church fends off the attacks of a defeated, persistent foe; a roaring, but toothless lion; a headless serpent whose wiggling tail seems so enticing.

St. Paul was aware of this struggle. Read some of his comments on this struggle for humanity's soul. Then answer the questions that follow.

1. **Ephesians 6:10-12:** Who are the **"rulers . . . authorities . . . the powers of this dark world . . . spiritual forces of evil in the heavenly realms"?**

_____

_____

2. **Romans 8:38-39:**
a. Who or what separates us from God's love?

_____

b. How does Satan try to separate you from God's love?

_____

_____

3. **Romans 7:14-25:**
a. Describe Paul's inward struggle.

_____

_____

b. When we have lost a skirmish, how can we still claim victory?

_____

_____

4. **2 Timothy 4:6-8:** What do you think Paul was facing? How did he feel about it?

_____

_____

SECOND HALF

1. The battle for your soul is not waged on some celestial battlefield. This struggle occurs on the battlefield of life in everyday situations. The enemy here has been described as Satan. However, Scripture indicates that Satan has help. It refers quite often to the "unholy three": *The devil, the world, the sinful flesh.*

Satan or the devil we have met. God mentions *the world* in **1 John 2:15-17,** and we read about our sinful flesh in **Galatians 5:17.** You probably meet the latter two most often. Satan does not appear in a red suit with a pitchfork. Rather, he often uses the sinful world and our own sinful flesh to tempt us to forsake Christ.

How easily can you discover the enemy? Following are some current hiding places of the "unholy three."

With your class or discussion group, explore each area as follows:

a. Divide the areas below into groups: **Temptations from the World** and **Temptations of the Sinful Flesh.** Some might fit under both headings.

b. List examples of how Satan uses those temptations to try to separate you from God's love.

Movies	Music	Fashions
TV	Education	Sex
Advertising	Food	Fame
Sports	Drugs	Success
Friends	Alcohol	Religion

2. You are living in a time when Satan also works directly. Describe the appeal some people find in the following:

Religions like Hinduism or Buddhism

Satan worship

"Being good" (trying to work our way into heaven)

3. Satan and his cohorts are powerful, formidable enemies. How can we resist their temptations? How can we remain God's sons and daughters after we succumb to them?

_____

_____

_____

_____

Our struggle is not against flesh and blood, but against the rulers, against the authorities, against the powers of this dark world and against the spiritual forces of evil in the heavenly realms.

Ephesians 6:12

SESSION 37

Using Your Equipment

WARM-UP

Have you heard about the first battle of Bull Run, one of the early battles of the Civil War? The Union army went into the battle completely sure of victory. Bull Run is quite close to Washington, D.C. Many federal government officials took the day off to ride out and watch the defeat of the Confederate army. Some husbands and wives looked upon the battle as entertainment for a picnic lunch.

But people from the North did not realize how determined the Confederate army was. Soon after the first shots were fired, it was clear who would win. The young, inexperienced, and poorly trained Union army was soon in retreat—actually more of a headlong panic. Spectators couldn't get away fast enough. They left picnic baskets, carriages, and chairs behind. Young Union recruits, running for their lives, threw down hats, coats, rifles, knapsacks—all their new equipment. At this point they just wanted to get out alive!

Experienced soldiers do not discard their equipment. They know that each piece has a purpose and is vital to their survival.

Experienced "called-out soldiers" in the army of the Lord know that, too. In fact their spiritual equipment is their most valuable possession. Read about this equipment in **Ephesians 6:13-18.**

FIRST HALF

St. Paul here describes the armor and equipment of a typical Roman soldier. As Paul sat in his own rented house in Rome, he merely had to look up and see how the equipment of the guard assigned to him was so much like the spiritual equipment God gives to each of His warriors.

1. Unlike the recruits of the Union army, Paul reminds us to wear the full armor of God. What might happen if a soldier decided not to wear a certain piece of equipment?

_____

_____

2. When is "the day of evil" for Christ's army?

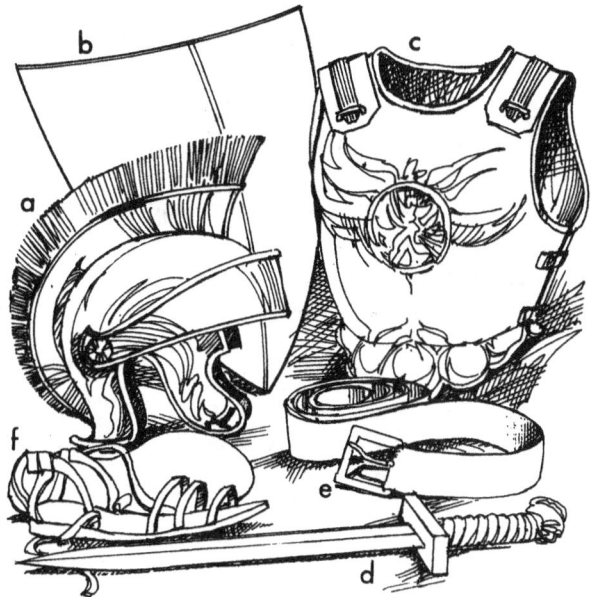

_____

_____

3. Why is mere "standing your ground" so important to Christ?

_____

_____

4. Look at the drawing of a typical Roman soldier. Label each piece indicated by number with the name Paul gives it.

a._____   d._____

b._____   e._____

c._____   f._____

Paul had a reason for labeling each piece of equipment as he did. Below are brief descriptions of how a Roman soldier used his equipment.

The Belt or girdle secured the undergarments and kept them from getting in the way during times of critical activity.

The breastplate, made of leather, protected vital organs from direct blows.

The helmet protected the warrior from losing consciousness from blows to the head.

The shield could skillfully be moved to ward off sword strokes or flying arrows.

Sandals were made of tough leather and enabled the warrior to travel over rough terrain.

The sword was the only offensive weapon. Soldiers could use it to disable and kill. Much practice was required to make its use effective.

5. Now let us discover the value of God's armor. Below are references that describe the value of each. After reading each description, write a statement comparing God's armor to the Roman armor. The first is done as an example.

a. *Truth:* **John 8:31-32.** (The truth that Jesus taught keeps us from being confused and hobbled by loose and dangling information.)

b. *Righteousness:* **Romans 3:21-24**

_____

_____

c. *The Gospel:* **Romans 1:16-17**

_____

_____

d. *Faith:* **Hebrews 11:1; Mark 11:12-14, 20-24**

_____

_____

e. *Salvation:* **1 John 3:1-3**

_____

_____

f. *Word of God:* **Matthew 4:1-11**

_____

_____

SECOND HALF

God has given you all the equipment you need. He also empowers you to use it. Below are some everyday battle situations. You probably recognize the enemy in each. As you prepare for battle in each instance, tell which piece(s) of equipment you would need and how you would use it (them).

1. You are told that "you only go around once; so grab all the gusto you can." Or "This life is all there is; so enjoy it."

2. Your friends put down anyone who goes to church or is a goody-goody.

3. You've had an entire week of disasters: two unexpected Fs; a cold; a broken romance; and being benched. You are ready to chuck it all in.

4. You got caught cheating red-handed. You've never done anything like this before. Your parents, teachers, and even your friends are shocked.

5. You are in a heated discussion with some unbelieving friends who are ridiculing Bible "stories," miracles, and "all the other kid stuff in the Bible."

6. Quite unexpectedly, a very quiet acquaintance at work comes up and asks, "How come you're so different from the other clowns who work here? You never blow your top or use bad language."

Put on the full armor of God, so that when the day of evil comes, you may be able to stand your ground, and after you have done everything, to stand.

Ephesians 6:13

SESSION 38

The Sword of the Spirit

WARM-UP

One of the more interesting discoveries about the equipment God issues to His soldiers concerns the **sword of the Spirit (Eph. 6:17).** Here are some of those discoveries.

1. Paul lists only the sword as an offensive weapon for the "called-out ones."

2. The church's symbol for St. Paul is a sword (*Spiritus gladius* in Latin), yet Paul probably never even owned a sword.

3. A sword is not like a Swiss army pocket knife. Soldiers use a sword for only one thing, to hurt and kill.

4. The sword was the weapon of a trained career officer. Spears and clubs were the weapons of the foot soldier.

The purpose of this session is to acquaint you with this offensive weapon, the **sword of the Spirit.** In doing this, we will explore the ideas behind the four discoveries presented above. Then we will understand how better to use it.

FIRST HALF
Matthew 4:1-17

Why did the Lord give us only one weapon to fight against Satan's temptations? Would it not be better to be armed to the teeth? To answer this question, we need go no farther than to the example of our Savior. Consider what He had at His disposal to fight against Satan. Look up these two references. Write what He could have used.

1. **Matthew 26:52-54**

_____

_____

2. **John 18:36**

_____

_____

Instead, Jesus used only God's Word, the same sword of the Spirit we use.

3. Read **Matthew 4:1-17.** What were the Old Testament references Jesus quoted?

a. _____

b. _____

c. _____

_____

4. What do you think would happen to us as soldiers if we could order angels around and work miracles on our own?

_____

_____

1 Corinthians 2

St. Paul probably never even owned a sword. Yet he was the first to use the term *Spiritus gladius,* sword of the Spirit. He was a master at using it. Read **1 Corinthians 2** and answer the following questions.

1. How do you know that the power in Paul's message was not in his speaking but in the Spirit?

_____

_____

2. How can mortal man understand what God has given us?

_____

_____

3. After reading this, why do you think the symbol for Paul is the sword of the Spirit?

_____

_____

Hebrews 4:12-13

The sword of the Spirit is mentioned again in **Hebrews 4:12-13**. Most Bible students believe **Hebrews** was written by an unknown Christian, and not by Paul. This writer describes the Word of God as **"sharper than any double-edged sword."** In ancient times a skillful swordsman could defend himself better with a two-edged sword. No matter which way he swung his sword, an edge of sharpened steel was presented.

As a spiritual weapon we recognize two cutting edges in God's Word. They are called *Law and Gospel.* Both are to be used to advance the cause of the kingdom. But they differ vastly from each other.

The Law:
a. always says what God wants us to do.
b. brings fear and frustration as we see that we have broken God's law and cannot keep it.
c. is used to expose sin, and thereby to show the need for a Savior, One who can save us from the demands of the Law.

The Gospel:
a. tells us what God has done to save us.
b. brings peace and joy as we see how Christ not only kept the Law for us, but also paid for every sin that we committed and will commit.
c. is used to comfort the hearts that have been devastated by the Law.

As we wield this sword, we use a power that Satan cannot defeat. One edge (the Law) exposes the temptations of Satan for what they are: lies that break God's law. The other edge (the Gospel) provides us with the power we have (God's love in Christ) to defeat Satan.

Look again at **Matthew 4:1-11** and the thrusts of the sword of the Spirit as used by Jesus. Write whether what He said was mostly Law or mostly Gospel.

1. **verse 4** _____

2. **verse 7** _____

3. **verse 10** _____

SECOND HALF

Among the challenges of the study and use of God's Word is that of properly using Law and Gospel. A first step is that of identifying Law and Gospel as they appear in Scripture.

1. Following are various quotes from the Old and New Testaments. Identify each as Law (L) or Gospel (G). Do not be misled by where the quote is. Many times we find Law and Gospel side by side.

a. ____ **John 3:16**

b. ____ **Matthew 5:3-10**

c. ____ **Matthew 5:38-39**

d. ____ **John 14:2-4**

e. ____ **Acts 2:36**

f. ____ **Isaiah 9:2**

g. ____ **Isaiah 9:19**

h. ____ **Ezekiel 34:1-4**

i. ____ **Ezekiel 34:11-16**

j. ____ **2 Peter 3:8-9**

k. ____ **2 Peter 3:10**

l. ____ **James 1:25**

m. ____ **Genesis 3:15**

n. ____ **Revelation 22:18-19**

2. Which statement of Law from the above list did you need to hear the most? Don't write it down. Just think about it. Then talk together about how the Law helps Christians today.

3. Which Gospel promise from the list means the most to you? Share your answer with one person in your class.

The word of God is living and active. Sharper than any double-edge sword, it penetrates even to dividing soul and spirit, joints and marrow; it judges the thoughts and attitudes of the heart.

Hebrews 4:12

SESSION 39

The Great Battle

WARM-UP

Have you ever wondered why coaches make you do all those little drills and exercises? When you are in the middle of one, no doubt many ideas come to mind—none too pleasant.

Actually, such drills and exercises have valuable purposes. Below are listed some sports and other activities with a typical drill from each. Can you come up with the ultimate purpose?

1. *Basketball:* running the lines
2. *Football:* grass drills
3. *Track:* interval training
4. *Language:* declining nouns
5. *Driving:* road test

You, no doubt, can think of many more. And in a serious moment, you also know that these pesky drills all have value. They prepare you for the real activity.

As you study God's Word, your teachers may require you to memorize passages, do work sheets, and take tests. These are not ends in themselves. They prepare you for something bigger—for the final struggle between the church and the forces of Satan. Like it or not, you are a part of it.

St. Paul was very aware of this struggle, as were all of the disciples. Let us first listen in as Christ Himself tells the disciples of this great struggle at the end of time.

FIRST HALF
Luke 21:5-19

From our vantage point we can understand that Jesus was telling His disciples what would happen to them after He has ascended to heaven.

1. **Verses 8-9:** How will Satan try to frighten and tear Christ's followers away?

_____

2. **Verse 12:** List some events from the **Book of Acts** that actually fulfilled these predictions. Page through **Acts 4, 6–8, 12, 21–26** to find examples.

_____

_____

3. **Verses 13-15:** How does Jesus describe how His disciples will use the sword of the Spirit?

_____

_____

4. **Verses 16-19:** Yet Jesus' soldiers will suffer losses. According to this, what are they?

_____

_____

5. Jesus' soldiers today still suffer losses. Show that this is true from your experience or from what you have heard.

_____

_____

2 Thessalonians 2:1-12

Paul here is writing to "called-out ones" who were confused by various false teachings about the great struggle at the end of time. He begins this section by referring to a letter supposedly written by Paul that stated that Jesus had already returned the second time, gathered His faithful to eternity, and returned to heaven. The Thessalonian Christians were afraid they had missed out.

Paul tells them that before Jesus returns again, a few frightening things will happen first.

1. **Verses 3, 4, 9-10:** What are some of the identifying marks of **"the man of lawlessness"**?

_____

_____

2. **Verse 8:** When Jesus does return, what will He use to finally defeat **"the lawless one"**?

_____

_____

3. How do you know from this entire reading that the final struggle will be a spiritual battle, and that the sword of the Spirit will be at its center?

_____

_____

4. As a class activity supply examples from events today of how Satan is attempting to deceive "called-out ones." You may be able to find examples in the *Church Ads* of a recent newspaper. In the space below list examples for each category. Feel free to add more categories.

a. **Revealing the future:**

_____

_____

b. **Working miracles:**

_____

_____

c. **Seeing visions:**

_____

_____

d. **Having success in life:**

_____

_____

e. **Learning secrets:**

_____

_____

SECOND HALF

In the space below write how you would respond to one of the deceptions discussed above. As you answer, remember that the **"sword of the Spirit"** is the only weapon we have to disarm Satan's lies. Use your Bible, its cross-references, and material from your text to help you formulate a defense. Above all, ask for divine guidance as you work. Be ready to read your response in the next session.

_____

_____

_____

_____

_____

_____

_____

Then the lawless one will be revealed, whom the Lord Jesus will overthrow with the breath of His mouth and destroy by the splendor of His coming.
2 Thessalonians 2:8

SESSION 40

Within the Grasp of Victory

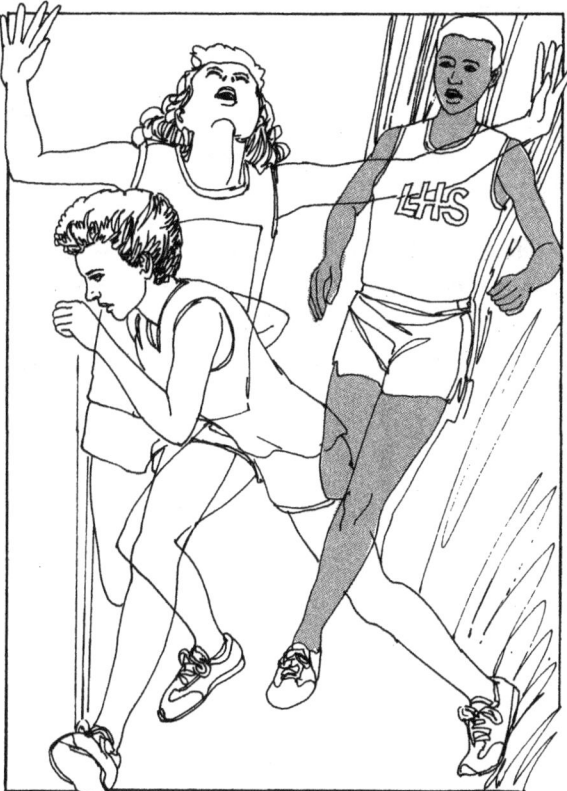

WARM-UP

Take time to share the ways people in your class responded to the attacks of Satan in session 39. As you listen, remember that these attacks come from within an organized local congregation. Many of Satan's most effective temptations come from the least likely sources.

Think of each of your classmates as a fellow warrior against a common enemy. As you listen, think of other ways to respond. Remember to be helpful, not critical, as you discuss these responses.

FIRST HALF

Having heard from each other, let us now hear from one of Christ's greatest warriors, St. Paul. In **Philip-** **pians 3:12—4:1** he summarizes his own battle in terms of a race in a track meet.

Following are some training and strategy techniques used in track and field. First read the words from Paul. Then write the number of the verse(s) in which Paul says the same thing about our spiritual contest. Track references do not necessarily follow the same sequence as presented by Paul.

1. _____Winning athletes follow the training rules of their coach and the examples of leading athletes on their team.

2. _____No athlete ever achieves perfection, but must train daily, always striving to win first place in the events for which he or she has been chosen.

3. _____Those who break training rules by drinking, smoking, and abusing their bodies are actually hurting the team and are really helping the opposition.

4. _____A mature athlete recognizes that there are differences in ability on a team. Such an athlete will let the coach decide who will run in which event, and will never give less than 100% in whatever event he or she is placed.

5. _____In a race the athlete never looks back, but always forward to the finish line.

6. _____Members of a winning team recognize that their training and physical conditioning have contributed to their success. They also appreciate the wonderful body their gracious God has given them.

SECOND HALF

Having compared Paul's words and the training requirements of track and field, let us now apply his words to our lives as "called-out ones." Write a personal answer to each of the following questions.

Philippians 3:12-14

1. When did Christ take hold of you and put you in the contest?

_____

2. In **3:7-11** Paul mentions that we receive our greatness—our hope for success in this contest—through Christ. In **Titus 3:4-7** he tells how baptism makes us heirs of eternal life. How does it help you, as you think of the contest you face, to remember your baptism daily?

_____

_____

3. What would happen to you if you had to remember every sin in order for Christ to forgive you?

_____

Philippians 3:15-16

How can you feel at one with a fellow "called-out one" who may worship or express faith differently than you do?

_____

_____

Philippians 3:17—4:1

1. What part of Christ's training program do you find the most difficult?

_____

2. When you finally reach the goal in eternity, what activity would you like to be able to do perfectly in order to express your gratitude to your Savior?

_____

_____

Perhaps your answer is what Paul is getting at in **4:1**. But you don't have to wait until heaven to get started. You can begin now already in standing firm, "doing your thing" for the Lord here and now.

Therefore, my brothers, you whom I love and long for, my joy and crown, that is how you should stand firm in the Lord, dear friends!

Philippians 4:1

SESSION 41

More than Conquerors

FINAL WHISTLE

What is it that makes stretching, drills, scrimmages, and conditioning all worthwhile? In the words of many coaches and players, "There is no substitute for winning!" Just the thought of how you feel in victory can often spur you on through even the most difficult practice.

Our Lord includes the declaration of victory in His messages for His church. From His side of eternity God declares us the winners over Satan, death, and our sinful flesh. What great news this is to those "called-out ones" slugging it out in the contest of everyday life!

In these last five sessions we will read what St. Paul wrote of God's great victory for us. Through these words God will help us enjoy the fruits of victory now and look forward to the eternal celebration in heaven.

To remind us that in Christ the victory is ours, the remaining sessions have a different format. We will leave the field of conflict and enter the winners' circle. Instead of "Warming Up" and competing in "First and Second Halves," we will begin each session with "Final Whistle" and continue with "Celebration."

CELEBRATION

Read **Romans 8:28-39** to see how Paul expressed his joy and confidence in Christ's victory for us. Then answer the following questions on your own. Later, be ready to share your responses with the class or your discussion group.

The Gospel

1. **Verse 32** is a clear expression of the pure Gospel. Rewrite this verse substituting nouns for all pronouns.

_____

_____

2. In **verses 33** and **34** Paul asks, **"Who will bring any charge . . . who is he that condemns?"** Who is it that raises these charges?

_____

3. Paul again presents pure Gospel as he answers these charges. Rephrase these two statements in your own words.

_____

_____

You have just done an exercise in using the *sword of the Spirit.* You were using the Gospel to disarm Satan. Christ's victory for us is the last thing Satan wants to hear!

For "Called-Out Ones"

1. In **verse 28** Paul assures us that all things work for good for "called-out ones." What name could also be used for this group?

_____

2. Look at **verses 29-30.** Paul names five distinct acts that God does for each of His sons and daughters. Fill in the blanks below in the proper order.

From eternity, God:

a. _____ us

b. _____ us

c. _____ us

d. _____ us

e. _____ us

3. These five acts are a chain. During our lifetime we experience only **c** and **d.** God did **a** and **b** before we were born. He will do **e** when we die. You know you can be certain of **c** and **d.** You can be just as certain of **a, b,** and **e.**

Below are definitions for each of the five terms. Write the term on the proper line. They are not in the correct order.

T _____ declares us not guilty.

F _____ knows us personally—by name and personality, defects and all.

H _____ gives us life eternally with Him.

A _____ planned beforehand that we will be His son or daughter.

I _____ works faith in our hearts through the Gospel.

4. Now arrange these five acts, along with the letter before each word, in the proper order. Those letters spell the means by which we know this is true.

F _____

A _____

I _____

T _____

H _____

This Is Sure!

1. In **verse 35** Paul lists another question. Before you answer it, read the verses that follow. How does Paul answer the question?

_____

_____

2. In **verse 35** Paul says that the devil uses trouble, hardship, persecution, famine, nakedness, danger, and sword to try to separate us from the love of God. Paul lists other things in **verses 38-39.** Write them in the first column below (**e** and **h** have been done for you).

a. _____: _____

b. _____: _____

c. _____: _____

d. _____: _____

e. present: no present-day event can cancel out Christ's victory for us.

f. _____: _____

g. _____: _____

h. height: God's presence knows no boundary.

i. _____: _____

j. _____: _____

3. What does Paul say about all of them?

_____

4. What items has Paul left out?

_____

5. From this list and from the way Paul expresses it, who or what can force God not to love you?

_____

6. Now go back to the list in 2 and supply a reason why each item cannot take God's love from you. Again, items **e** and **h** have been done as examples.

7. Finally, share your answers with your class or members of your discussion group.

8. As you conclude your discussion, talk about the reason why Paul never in this text uses a singular pronoun for himself or his readers.

In all these things we are more than conquerors through Him who loved us. For I am convinced that . . . [nothing] will be able to separate us from the love of God that is in Christ Jesus our Lord.
Romans 8:37-39

SESSION 42

Swallowing Death

FINAL WHISTLE

The Scene: a small cell in a first-century Roman prison. A small, frail man stands peering off into the darkness. A younger man writing on a large piece of parchment is seated on a crude stool.

The writer is a Greek physician, Luke. The man dictating his last letter is Paul, the apostle. The letter is addressed to Paul's young friend, Timothy. Listen as the words flow from heart to paper.

"I am already being poured out like a drink offering, and the time has come for my departure. I have fought the good fight, I have finished the race, I have kept the faith. Now there is in store for me the crown of righteousness, which the Lord, the righteous Judge, will award me on that day—and not only to me, but also to all who have longed for His appearing" (2 Timothy 4:6-8).

Does this scene call for sniffles as the tears creep close to the surface? A Hollywood director might use sad music for it. But for those who can see beyond the cell and the gloom, this is a scene of victory. This is the beginning of a homecoming celebration. This is the final preparation before Paul would stand before his beloved Lord and Savior and hear from Him, "Well done, My faithful servant!"

In spite of his impending execution, Paul looked with longing to the glorious reunion in heaven with his Savior. For Paul, death was but a step into life.

CELEBRATION
Christ Defeats Death

Below are references to both Old and New Testament accounts of the history of death and its defeat. Read each reference. Then match it with the statement in the list that follows that summarizes a truth from the reference. All references will be used once. They outline how Christ has defeated death.

   a. **John 11:17-43**
   b. **1 Thessalonians 4:13-18**
   c. **Revelation 20:11-15**
   d. **Genesis 2:17; 3:6**
   e. **Genesis 3:15, 19, 22**

   f. **Genesis 4:2-8**
   g. **Genesis 5:3-31**
   h. **Daniel 12:2**
   i. **Matthew 27:45-54**
   j. **Luke 24:1-8**
   k. **1 Corinthians 15:12-23**
   l. **1 Corinthians 15:55-57**
   Summary Statements

1. ____ Adam and Eve disobey God's command and eat of the forbidden tree. Now they will die both in spirit and in body.

2. ____ God promises to send a Savior from eternal death. But yet all people will experience death of the body that was originally intended to live forever.

3. ____ Abel is killed and becomes the first to suffer bodily death.

4. ____ The curse of death continues as each

89

generation, with one exception, eventually falls under the pall of bodily death.

5. ____ The prophet is told that at the end of time all people will rise from the dust of death, some to eternal life, others to eternal separation from God.

6. ____ Just before His own death, Jesus raises Lazarus from the dead, a prelude to greater things to come.

7. ____ Jesus, as true God and as true man, suffers both separation from God and the death of the body.

8. ____ Jesus breaks the power of death by rising from the dead, as announced by two angels.

9. ____ Christ was the first to defeat death; now all of His followers will also rise in the great resurrection.

10. ____ Death, like a bee without a sting, holds no more terror for "called-out ones," for Christ has absorbed the sting of death.

11. ____ When a fellow "called-out one" dies, we can comfort the mourners with news that on the Last Day God will bring with Jesus those who have fallen asleep in Him.

12. ____ The final victory occurs when death is forever banished to hell, and the "called-out ones," whose names are so listed, will live forever with God in heaven.

Facing Death Today

Knowing that Christ has removed the terror of death for "called-out ones," write 200–300 words on one of the topics below or on one of your own.

1. Explaining Death to a Child
2. How Today's Society Covers Up Death
3. What My Funeral Will Be Like
4. What I Would Say to My Best Friend Whose Mother Died
5. The Differences Between Spiritual and Bodily Death

Christ has indeed been raised from the dead, the firstfruits of those who have fallen asleep.
1 Corinthians 15:20

SESSION 43

The Church at Home

FINAL WHISTLE

God did not provide a picture of heaven through Paul. Paul did, however, write about how the church would someday join Jesus Christ in glory. You might remember this description in **Ephesians 5:25-27.** We read this in session 27 as an analogy of how husbands are to love their wives. Now, in the context of the church celebrating the victory over sin, death, and Satan, let us read it once more.

"Husbands, love your wives, just as Christ loved the church and gave Himself up for her to make her holy, cleansing her by the washing with water through the word, and to present her to Himself as a radiant church, without stain or wrinkle or any other blemish, but holy and blameless."

Paul pictures the church as Christ's bride. She is radiant with beauty, clothed in the righteousness of God, holy and blameless. This is a perfect picture of each "called-out one" as a member of the church in glory.

St. John, in **Revelation 21,** repeats this analogy of the church being the bride of Christ. He expands the analogy and refers to the church as the New Jerusalem, the holy city **"prepared as a bride beautifully dressed for her husband" (v.2).**

We may be surprised to discover that Scripture says very little to describe our future life in heaven, though we do find a detailed description in **Revelation 21:1—22:5.** Perhaps God says so little because He does not want us to yearn for an eternal vacation in heaven. Jesus mentions something even better in **John 17:24: "Father, I want those you have given Me to be with Me where I am, and to see My glory."** The greatest attraction of heaven is to be with Jesus forever.

One part of Jesus' glory for the church is for us to dwell in everlasting happiness. To discover what this life will be like, read **Revelation 21:1—22:5.** Since John uses the analogy of the New Jerusalem for the church, we will look at this life as a home buyer would look at a real-estate report.

Fill in the questionnaire below with your teacher as the real-estate agent who will explain the exciting features of your new home! Use **Revelation 21:1—22:5** as a source of information.

CELEBRATION: REAL-ESTATE REPORT

Persons and Property Involved

1. Agent: _____

2. Prospective occupants: _____

3. Date of filing: _____

4. Date of possible occupancy: _____

5. Name of dwelling: _____

6. Location: _____

7. Age of structure: _____

8. Builder and developer: _____

9. Will owner live with occupant? _____

10. What environmental hazards are excluded?

_____

_____

11. What individuals are excluded?_____

_____

_____

Description of Property

1. Exterior appearance: _____

_____

2. Number of doors: _____

3. Number and identification of foundations: _____

_____

4. Measurements: _____

5. Construction materials: _____

_____

_____

Description of Amenities

1. Proximity to worship center: _____

2. Lighting: _____

3. Water supply: _____

4. Vegetation and food availability: _____

_____

5. Medical facilities: _____

Terms

1. Terms of tenancy: _____

_____

2. Asking price: _____

_____

3. Selling price: _____

_____

4. Down payment: _____

_____

5. Monthly payments: _____

_____

6. Name of buyer: _____

7. Beneficiary: _____

I saw the Holy City, the new Jerusalem, coming down out of heaven from God, prepared as a bride beautifully dressed for her husband.

Revelation 21:2

SESSION 44

A Victory Party

FINAL WHISTLE

This is actually the final whistle! Instruction and practice are over. The Holy Spirit through the writings of St. Paul has led you through a study of the community of "called-out ones"—the church.

The activities in this session will give you and your classmates an opportunity to celebrate in worship all that God has done for you in Christ. Even though, as we have seen, the real celebration will take place in heaven, our worship here together can be a beginning.

As you prepare for this celebration, plan a contribution you can make to the sacrificial part of the worship. (You may remember that the sacrificial part of worship is the part where "called-out ones" give of themselves to the Lord.) Your gift in this worship will be a short statement of what you plan to do later in your life—after you are finished with school. Then state how you can use your occupation as a witness to the world.

You might also wish to add a few words of how you feel about your fellow "called-out ones" now. Name them if you wish. Remember, one of the purposes of the church is to build each other up in the faith. Try to do that through your statement.

CELEBRATION

The Order of Worship

1. **Meditation:** Quietly think about your relationship with God and write a statement about being a "called-out one" now and in the future.
2. **Invocation: Philippians 1:1b-2** (with changes in names and titles)
3. **Hymn of Praise from the Past: Philippians 2:6-11** (to be read together)
4. **Hymns of Praise from the Future** (to be read by individuals)

    a. **Revelation 1:4b-6**
    b. **Revelation 1:7**
    c. **Revelation 5:9b-14**
    d. **Revelation 7:11-17**
    e. **Revelation 19:6-8**
    f. **Revelation 22:17**

5. **Epistle Reading: Ephesians 4:1-16**
Response (spoken by all): **Worthy is the Lamb, who was slain, to receive power and wealth and wisdom and strength and honor and glory and praise! (Revelation 5:12)**
6. **Gospel Reading: John 15:1-17**
Response (spoken by all): **To Him who sits on the throne and to the Lamb be praise and honor and glory and power, forever and ever! (Revelation 5:13)**
7. **Sounds of Heaven**
    a. Recording of "Hallelujah Chorus"
    b. Readings of statements
8. **Circle Prayer**
9. **Lord's Prayer**
10. **Benediction of St. Paul**
Peace to the brothers, and love with faith from God the Father and the Lord Jesus Christ. Grace to all who love our Lord Jesus Christ with an undying love (Ephesians 6:23-24).

SESSION 45

Concluding Activities for Unit 6

Take a few minutes to review concepts for unit 6.

Use these questions to help you describe the conflict we have with Satan and the victory that is ours through Christ. Write your answers on a separate sheet of paper.

1. Describe the battle for our souls that has occurred between Satan and God.

2. What spiritual armor does God provide for your battle against Satan? How do the various pieces of this armor help you?

3. How are Law and Gospel like the two edges of God's sword of the Spirit?

4. What are some of the devices Satan will use to try to deceive you?

5. Compare your struggle against Satan with training and technique facts from track and field.

6. What are the five eternal acts of love that St. Paul mentions in **Romans 8?** How do these acts that God did for you make you more confident of your salvation?

7. Summarize how God through Jesus Christ has defeated death.

8. Describe what life will be like in heaven. What will be the best thing about that life?

9. Which is your favorite song of victory from **Revelation?** Why?

10. What changes in your Christian faith have you noticed during this course?

11. What would you tell someone to let this person know what you believe about Jesus Christ and how He affects your life?

May the grace of the Lord Jesus Christ, and the love of God, and the fellowship of the Holy Spirit be with you all.

2 Corinthians 13:14

www.ingramcontent.com/pod-product-compliance
Lightning Source LLC
Chambersburg PA
CBHW081634040426
42449CB00014B/3313